CHAPTER

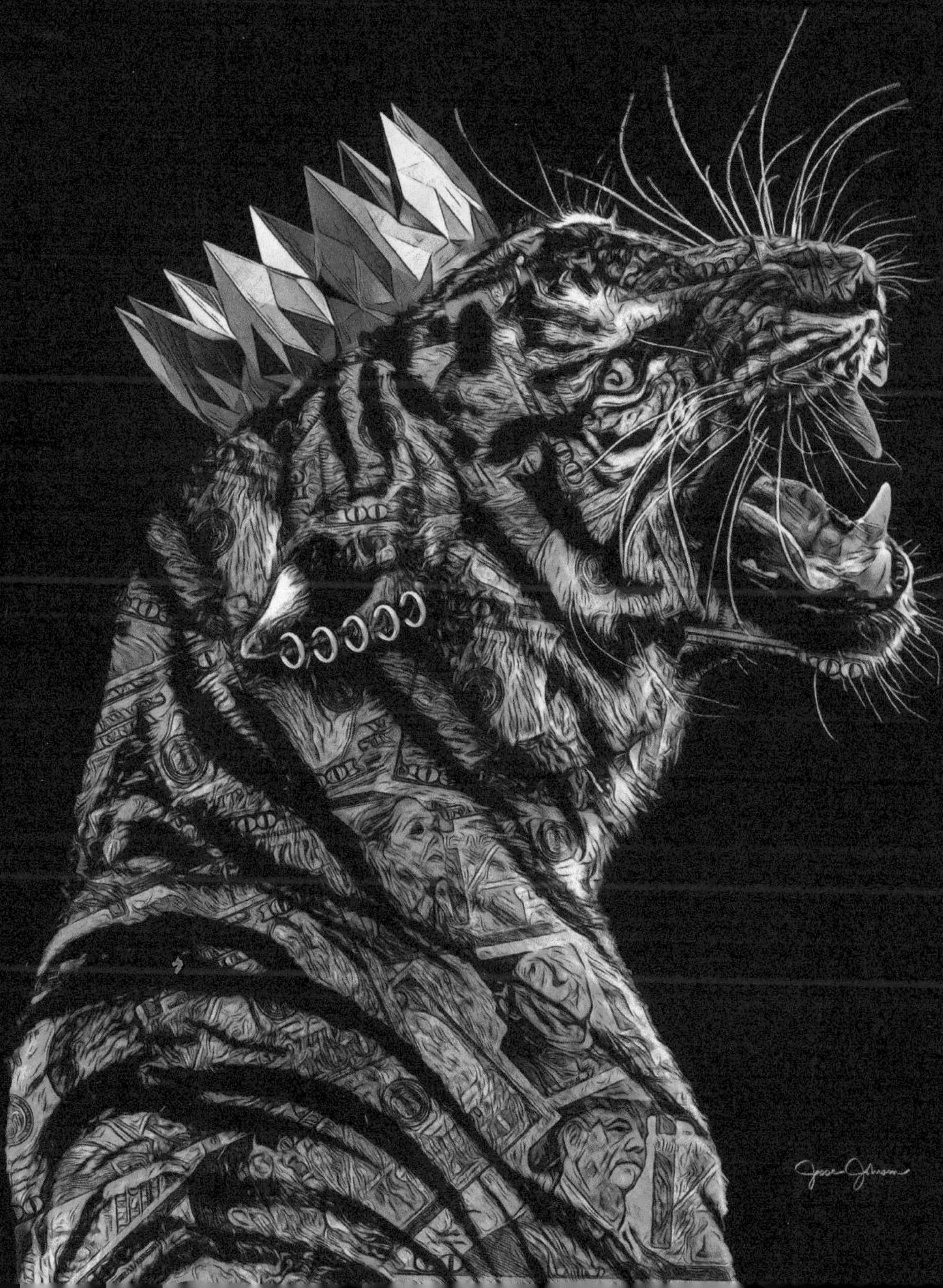

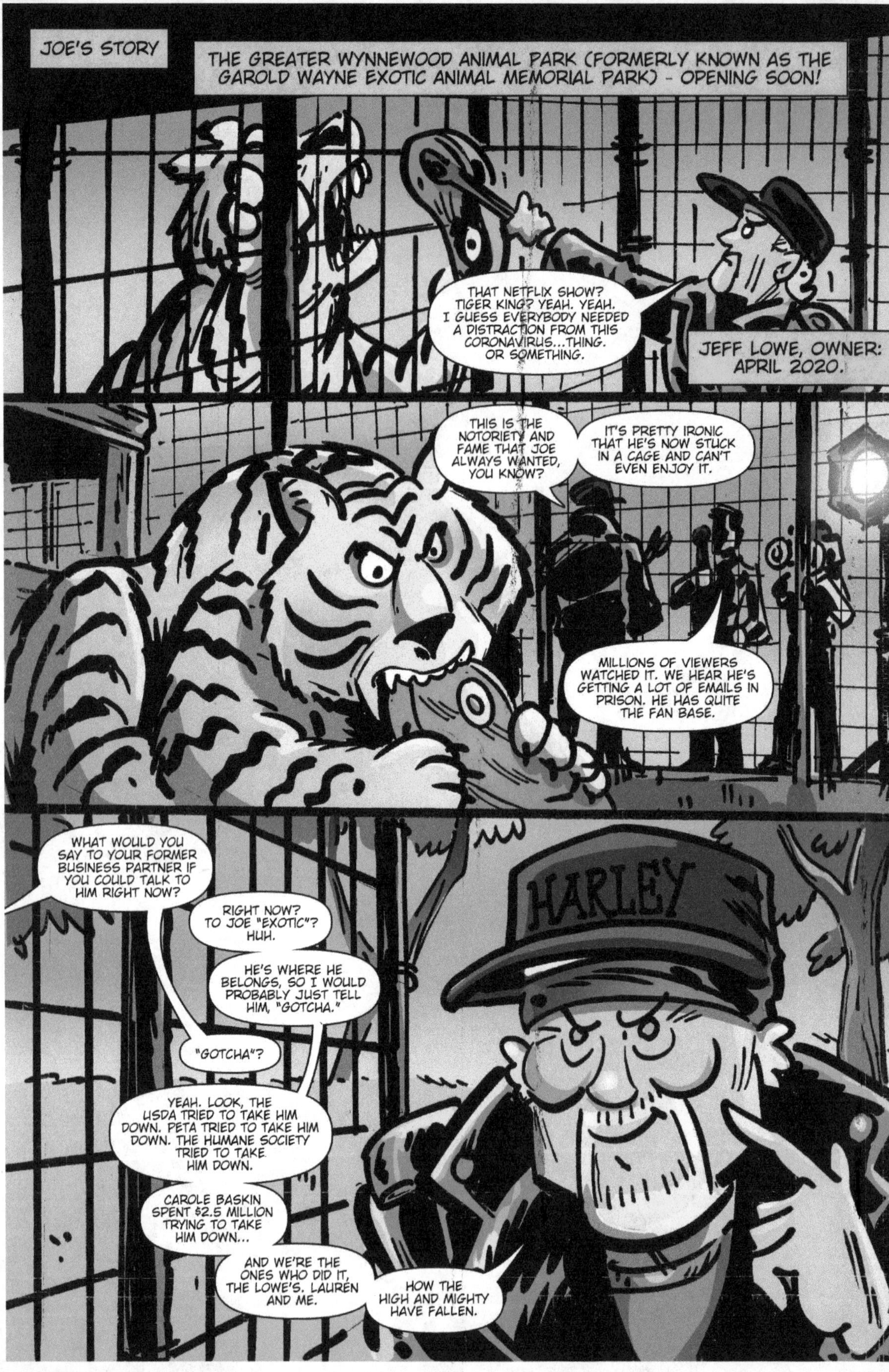
JOE'S STORY
THE GREATER WYNNEWOOD ANIMAL PARK (FORMERLY KNOWN AS THE GAROLD WAYNE EXOTIC ANIMAL MEMORIAL PARK) - OPENING SOON!
THAT NETFLIX SHOW? TIGER KING? YEAH. YEAH. I GUESS EVERYBODY NEEDED A DISTRACTION FROM THIS CORONAVIRUS...THING. OR SOMETHING.
JEFF LOWE, OWNER: APRIL 2020.
THIS IS THE NOTORIETY AND FAME THAT JOE ALWAYS WANTED, YOU KNOW?
IT'S PRETTY IRONIC THAT HE'S NOW STUCK IN A CAGE AND CAN'T EVEN ENJOY IT.
MILLIONS OF VIEWERS WATCHED IT. WE HEAR HE'S GETTING A LOT OF EMAILS IN PRISON. HE HAS QUITE THE FAN BASE.
WHAT WOULD YOU SAY TO YOUR FORMER BUSINESS PARTNER IF YOU COULD TALK TO HIM RIGHT NOW?
HARLEY
RIGHT NOW? TO JOE "EXOTIC"? HUH.
HE'S WHERE HE BELONGS, SO I WOULD PROBABLY JUST TELL HIM, "GOTCHA."
"GOTCHA"?
YEAH. LOOK, THE USDA TRIED TO TAKE HIM DOWN. PETA TRIED TO TAKE HIM DOWN. THE HUMANE SOCIETY TRIED TO TAKE HIM DOWN.
CAROLE BASKIN SPENT $2.5 MILLION TRYING TO TAKE HIM DOWN...
AND WE'RE THE ONES WHO DID IT, THE LOWE'S. LAUREN AND ME.
HOW THE HIGH AND MIGHTY HAVE FALLEN.

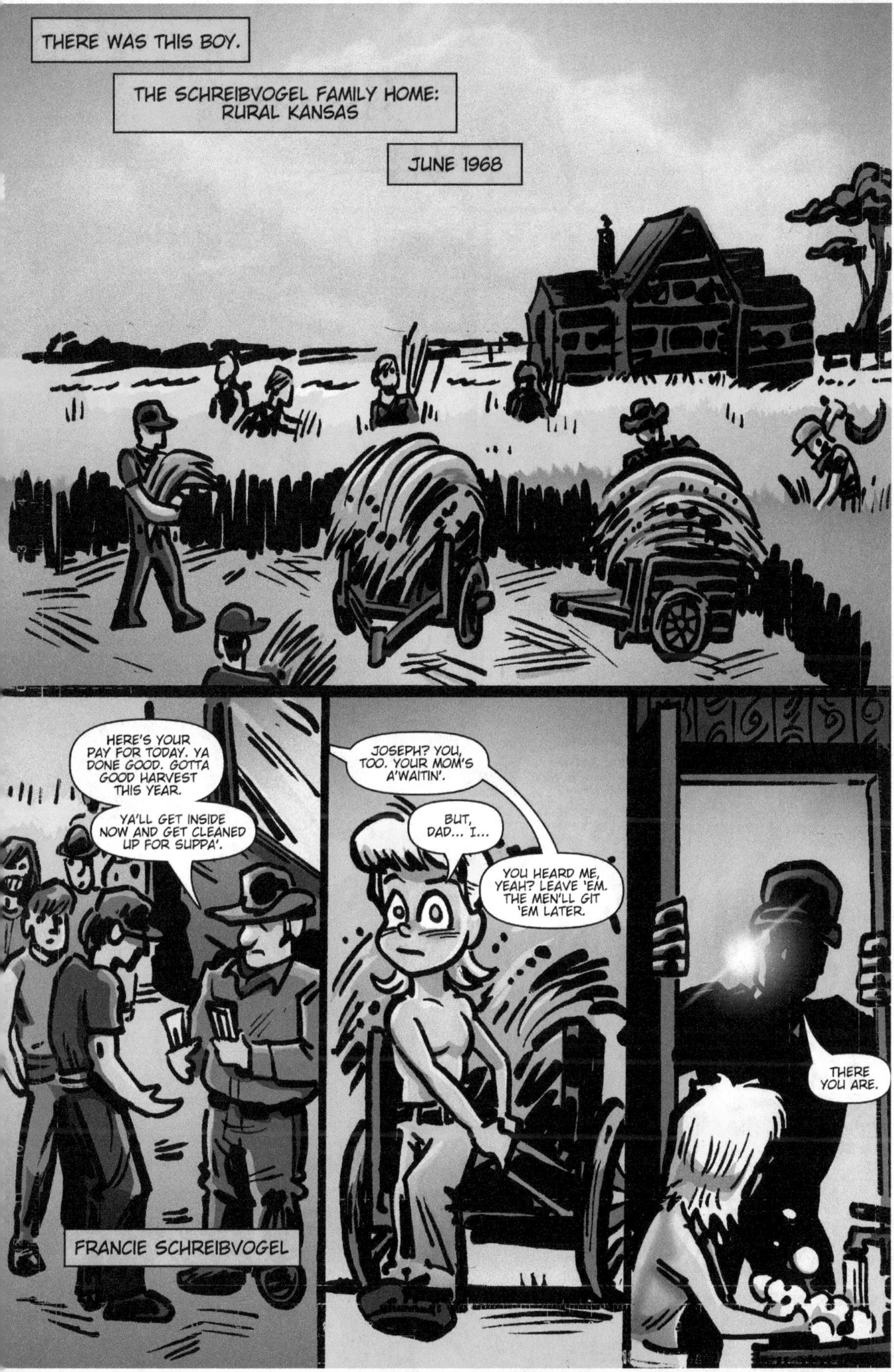
THERE WAS THIS BOY.
THE SCHREIBVOGEL FAMILY HOME: RURAL KANSAS
JUNE 1968
HERE'S YOUR PAY FOR TODAY. YA DONE GOOD. GOTTA GOOD HARVEST THIS YEAR.
YA'LL GET INSIDE NOW AND GET CLEANED UP FOR SUPPA'.
FRANCIE SCHREIBVOGEL
JOSEPH? YOU, TOO. YOUR MOM'S A'WAITIN'.
BUT, DAD... I...
YOU HEARD ME, YEAH? LEAVE 'EM. THE MEN'LL GIT 'EM LATER.
THERE YOU ARE.

GET ON OUTTA HERE. DINNER'S WAITIN'.
YEAH? WELL, DON'T YOU WANT ME TO GIT CLEAN FOR THE TABLE?
'SIDES, I WORKED HARD TODAY. REAL HARD.
GOTTA GET MY PAY FOR A JOB WELL DONE, YEAH?
SQUINK
GONNA BE A GREAT HARVEST THIS YEAR. YESSIR.

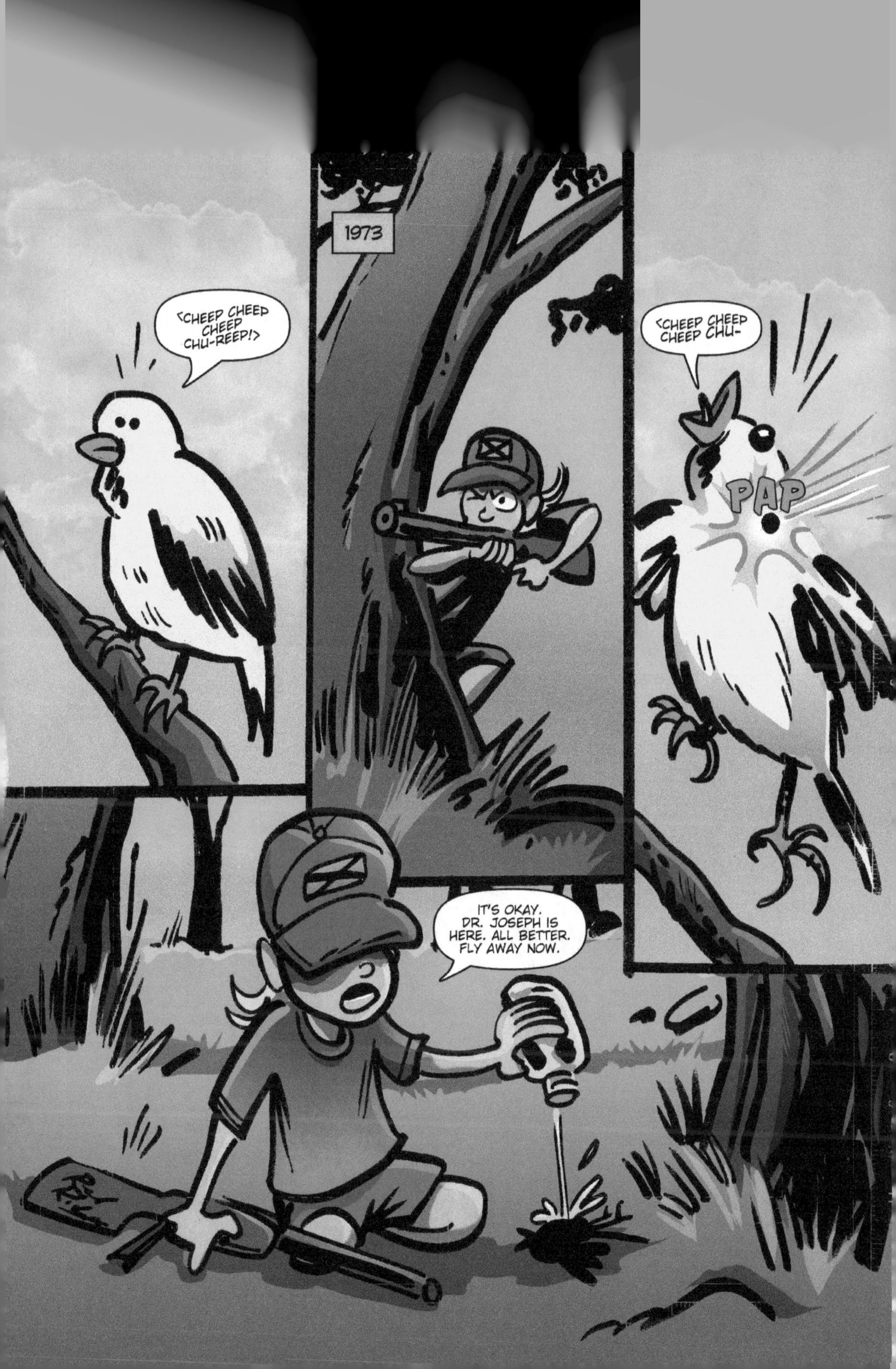
<CHEEP CHEEP CHEEP CHU-REEP!>
1973
<CHEEP CHEEP CHEEP CHU-
PAP
IT'S OKAY. DR. JOSEPH IS HERE. ALL BETTER. FLY AWAY NOW.

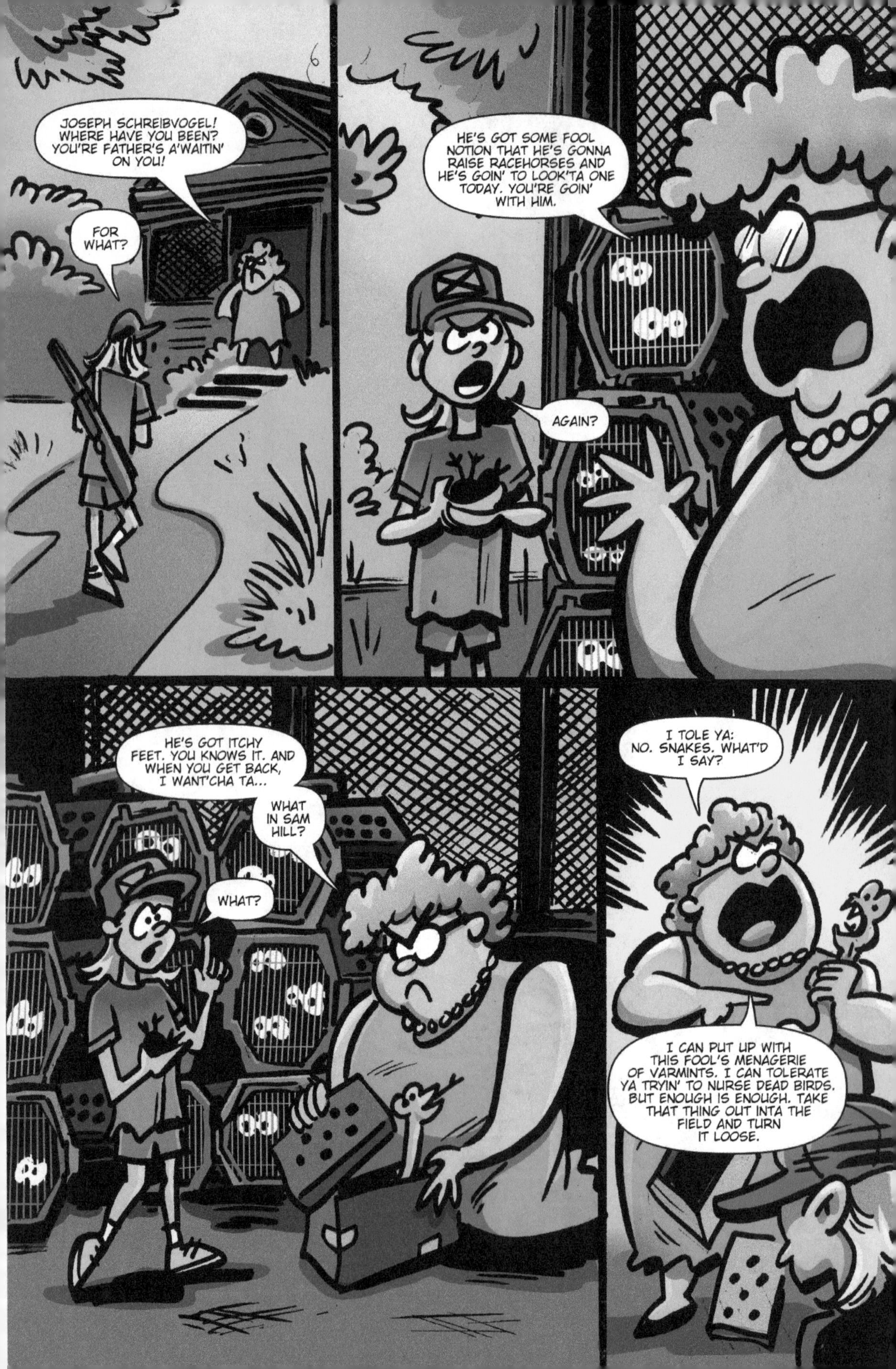
JOSEPH SCHREIBVOGEL! WHERE HAVE YOU BEEN? YOU'RE FATHER'S A'WAITIN' ON YOU!
FOR WHAT?
HE'S GOT SOME FOOL NOTION THAT HE'S GONNA RAISE RACEHORSES AND HE'S GOIN' TO LOOK'TA ONE TODAY. YOU'RE GOIN' WITH HIM.
AGAIN?
HE'S GOT ITCHY FEET. YOU KNOWS IT. AND WHEN YOU GET BACK, I WANT'CHA TA...
WHAT IN SAM HILL?
WHAT?
I TOLE YA: NO. SNAKES. WHAT'D I SAY?
I CAN PUT UP WITH THIS FOOL'S MENAGERIE OF VARMINTS. I CAN TOLERATE YA TRYIN' TO NURSE DEAD BIRDS. BUT ENOUGH IS ENOUGH. TAKE THAT THING OUT INTA THE FIELD AND TURN IT LOOSE.

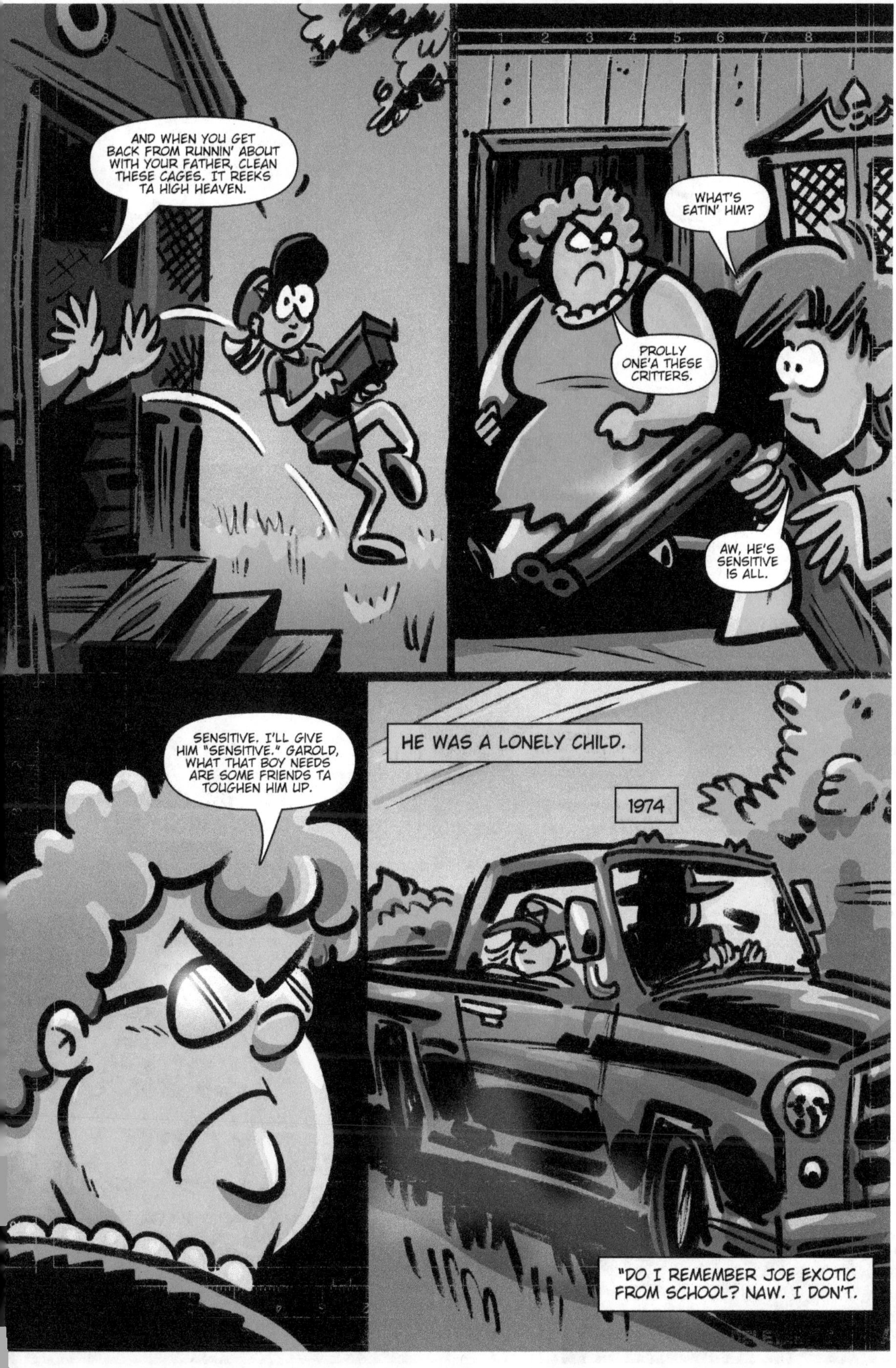
AND WHEN YOU GET BACK FROM RUNNIN' ABOUT WITH YOUR FATHER, CLEAN THESE CAGES. IT REEKS TA HIGH HEAVEN.
WHAT'S EATIN' HIM?
PROLLY ONE'A THESE CRITTERS.
AW, HE'S SENSITIVE IS ALL.
SENSITIVE. I'LL GIVE HIM "SENSITIVE." GAROLD, WHAT THAT BOY NEEDS ARE SOME FRIENDS TA TOUGHEN HIM UP.
HE WAS A LONELY CHILD.
1974
"DO I REMEMBER JOE EXOTIC FROM SCHOOL? NAW. I DON'T.

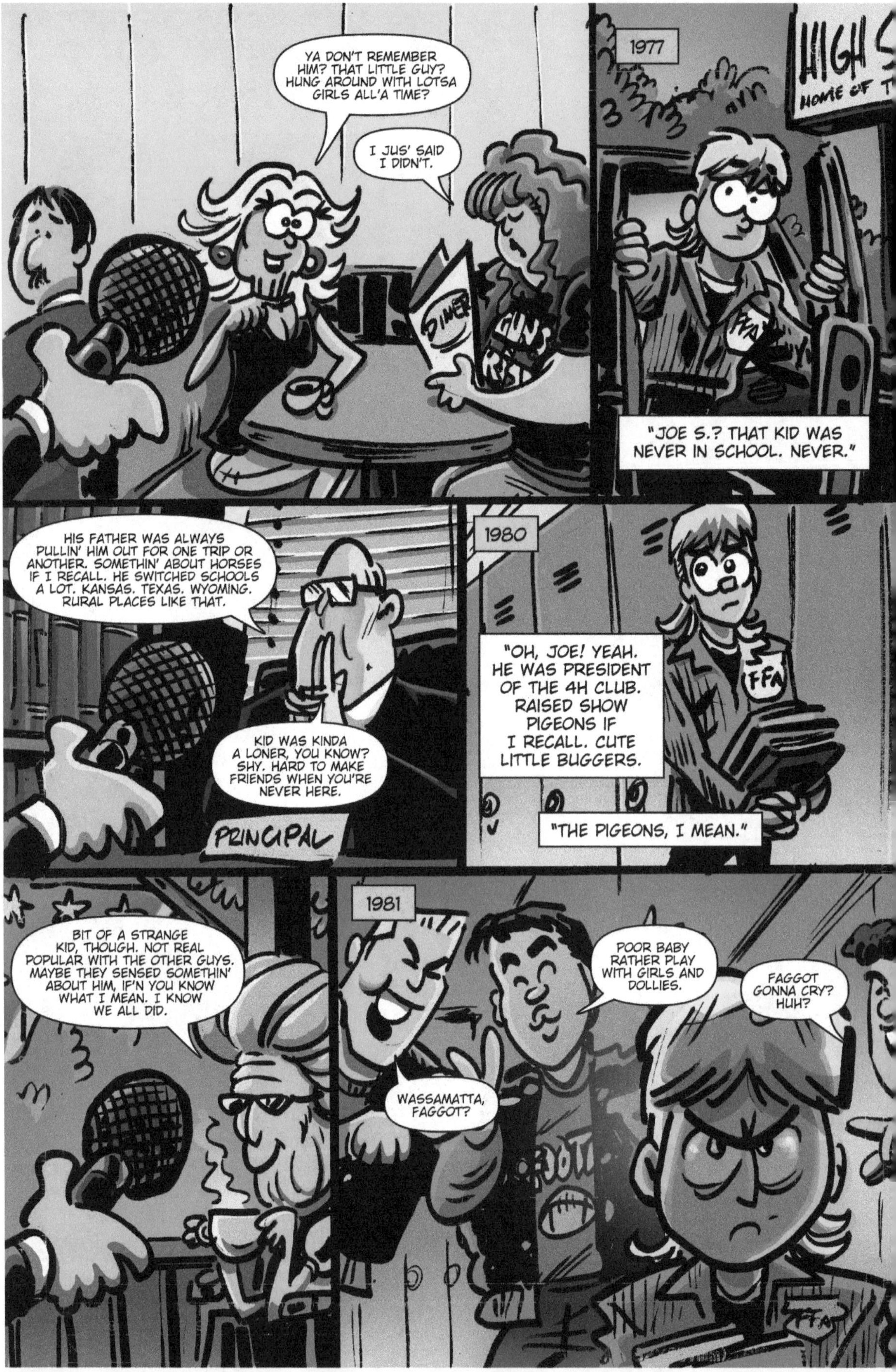
YA DON'T REMEMBER HIM? THAT LITTLE GUY? HUNG AROUND WITH LOTSA GIRLS ALL'A TIME?
I JUS' SAID I DIDN'T.
1977
"JOE S.? THAT KID WAS NEVER IN SCHOOL. NEVER."
HIS FATHER WAS ALWAYS PULLIN' HIM OUT FOR ONE TRIP OR ANOTHER. SOMETHIN' ABOUT HORSES IF I RECALL. HE SWITCHED SCHOOLS A LOT. KANSAS. TEXAS. WYOMING. RURAL PLACES LIKE THAT.
KID WAS KINDA A LONER, YOU KNOW? SHY. HARD TO MAKE FRIENDS WHEN YOU'RE NEVER HERE.
PRINCIPAL
1980
"OH, JOE! YEAH. HE WAS PRESIDENT OF THE 4H CLUB. RAISED SHOW PIGEONS IF I RECALL. CUTE LITTLE BUGGERS.
"THE PIGEONS, I MEAN."
BIT OF A STRANGE KID, THOUGH. NOT REAL POPULAR WITH THE OTHER GUYS. MAYBE THEY SENSED SOMETHIN' ABOUT HIM, IF'N YOU KNOW WHAT I MEAN. I KNOW WE ALL DID.
1981
WASSAMATTA, FAGGOT?
POOR BABY RATHER PLAY WITH GIRLS AND DOLLIES.
FAGGOT GONNA CRY? HUH?

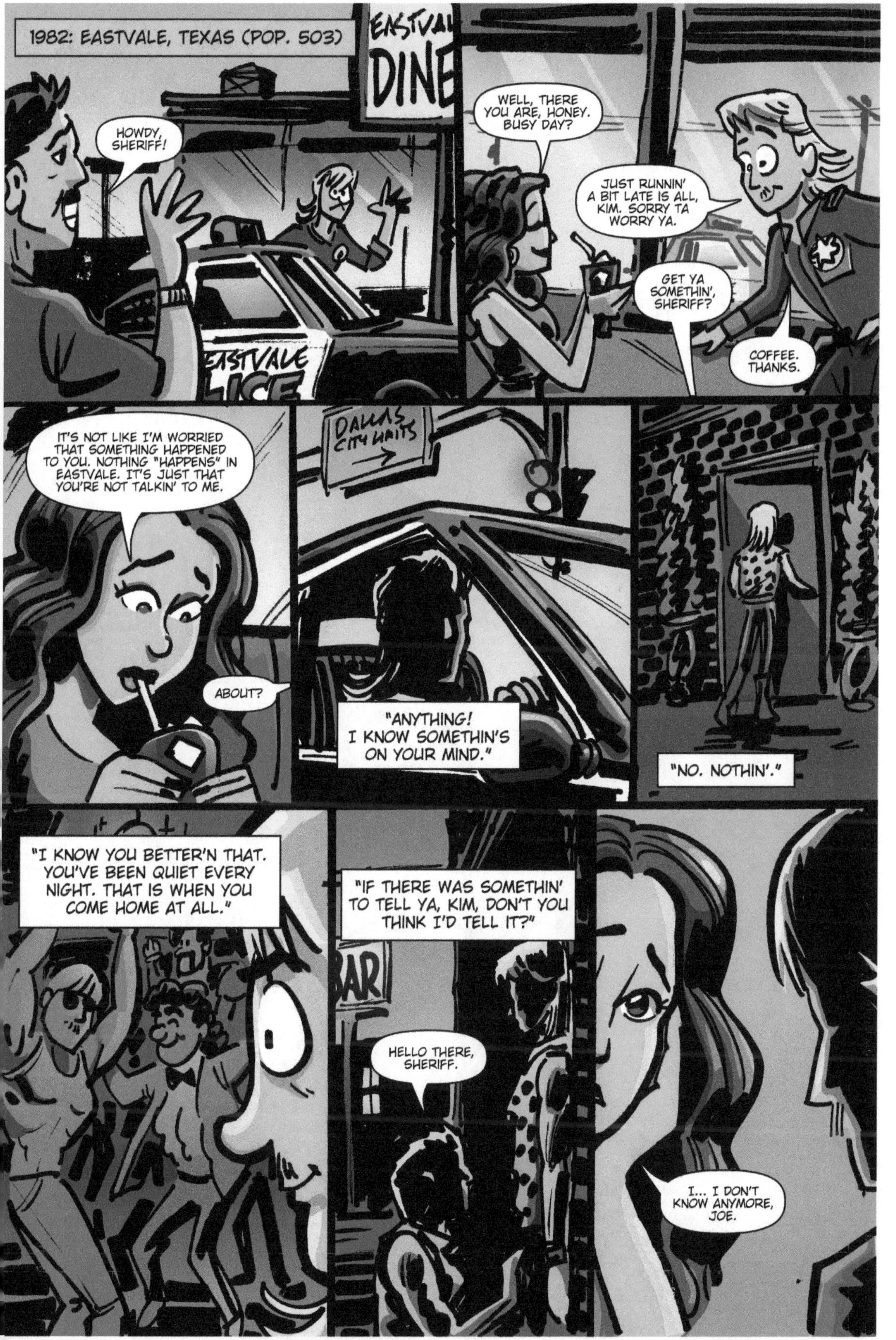
1982: EASTVALE, TEXAS (POP. 503)
EASTVALE DINE
HOWDY, SHERIFF!
EASTVALE LICE
WELL, THERE YOU ARE, HONEY. BUSY DAY?
JUST RUNNIN' A BIT LATE IS ALL, KIM. SORRY TA WORRY YA.
GET YA SOMETHIN', SHERIFF?
COFFEE. THANKS.
IT'S NOT LIKE I'M WORRIED THAT SOMETHING HAPPENED TO YOU. NOTHING "HAPPENS" IN EASTVALE. IT'S JUST THAT YOU'RE NOT TALKIN' TO ME.
ABOUT?
DALLAS CITY LIMITS
"ANYTHING! I KNOW SOMETHIN'S ON YOUR MIND."
"NO. NOTHIN'."
"I KNOW YOU BETTER'N THAT. YOU'VE BEEN QUIET EVERY NIGHT. THAT IS WHEN YOU COME HOME AT ALL."
"IF THERE WAS SOMETHIN' TO TELL YA, KIM, DON'T YOU THINK I'D TELL IT?"
BAR
HELLO THERE, SHERIFF.
I... I DON'T KNOW ANYMORE, JOE.

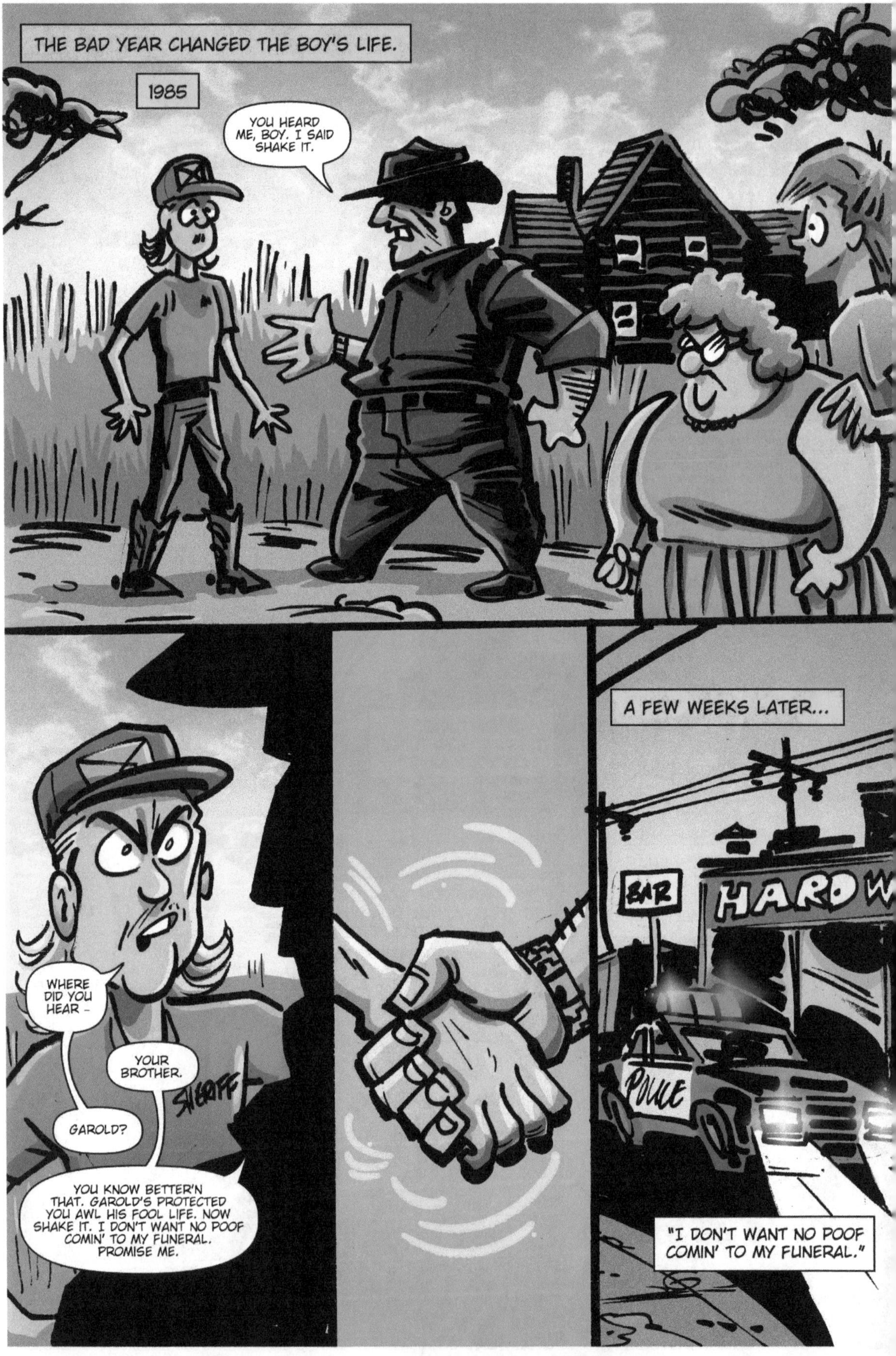

THE BAD YEAR CHANGED THE BOY'S LIFE.
1985
YOU HEARD ME, BOY. I SAID SHAKE IT.
WHERE DID YOU HEAR –
YOUR BROTHER.
GAROLD?
YOU KNOW BETTER'N THAT. GAROLD'S PROTECTED YOU AWL HIS FOOL LIFE. NOW SHAKE IT. I DON'T WANT NO POOF COMIN' TO MY FUNERAL. PROMISE ME.
SHERIFF
A FEW WEEKS LATER...
BAR
HARD
POLICE
"I DON'T WANT NO POOF COMIN' TO MY FUNERAL."

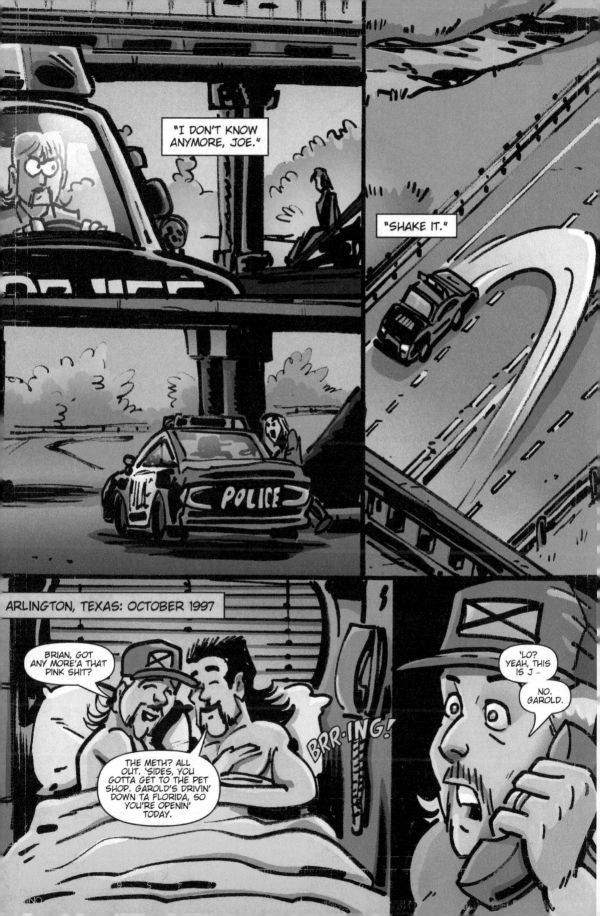

"I DON'T KNOW ANYMORE, JOE."

"SHAKE IT."

POLICE

ARLINGTON, TEXAS: OCTOBER 1997

BRIAN, GOT ANY MORE'A THAT PINK SHIT?

THE METH? ALL OUT. 'SIDES, YOU GOTTA GET TO THE PET SHOP. GAROLD'S DRIVIN' DOWN TA FLORIDA, SO YOU'RE OPENIN' TODAY.

BRR-ING!

'LO? YEAH, THIS IS J —

NO. GAROLD.

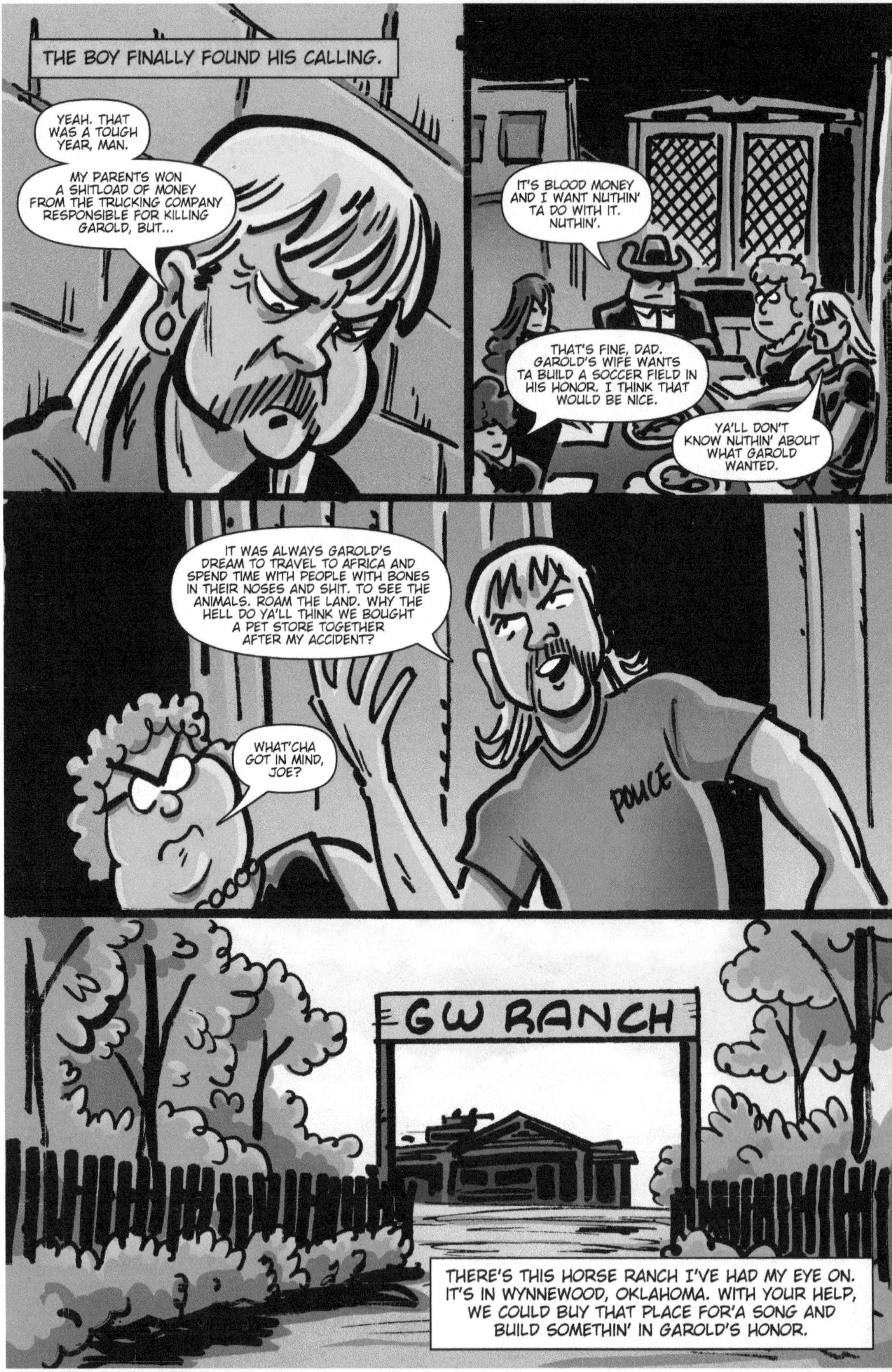
THE BOY FINALLY FOUND HIS CALLING.
YEAH. THAT WAS A TOUGH YEAR, MAN.
MY PARENTS WON A SHITLOAD OF MONEY FROM THE TRUCKING COMPANY RESPONSIBLE FOR KILLING GAROLD, BUT...
IT'S BLOOD MONEY AND I WANT NUTHIN' TA DO WITH IT. NUTHIN'.
THAT'S FINE, DAD. GAROLD'S WIFE WANTS TA BUILD A SOCCER FIELD IN HIS HONOR. I THINK THAT WOULD BE NICE.
YA'LL DON'T KNOW NUTHIN' ABOUT WHAT GAROLD WANTED.
IT WAS ALWAYS GAROLD'S DREAM TO TRAVEL TO AFRICA AND SPEND TIME WITH PEOPLE WITH BONES IN THEIR NOSES AND SHIT. TO SEE THE ANIMALS. ROAM THE LAND. WHY THE HELL DO YA'LL THINK WE BOUGHT A PET STORE TOGETHER AFTER MY ACCIDENT?
WHAT'CHA GOT IN MIND, JOE?
POLICE
GW RANCH
THERE'S THIS HORSE RANCH I'VE HAD MY EYE ON. IT'S IN WYNNEWOOD, OKLAHOMA. WITH YOUR HELP, WE COULD BUY THAT PLACE FOR'A SONG AND BUILD SOMETHIN' IN GAROLD'S HONOR.

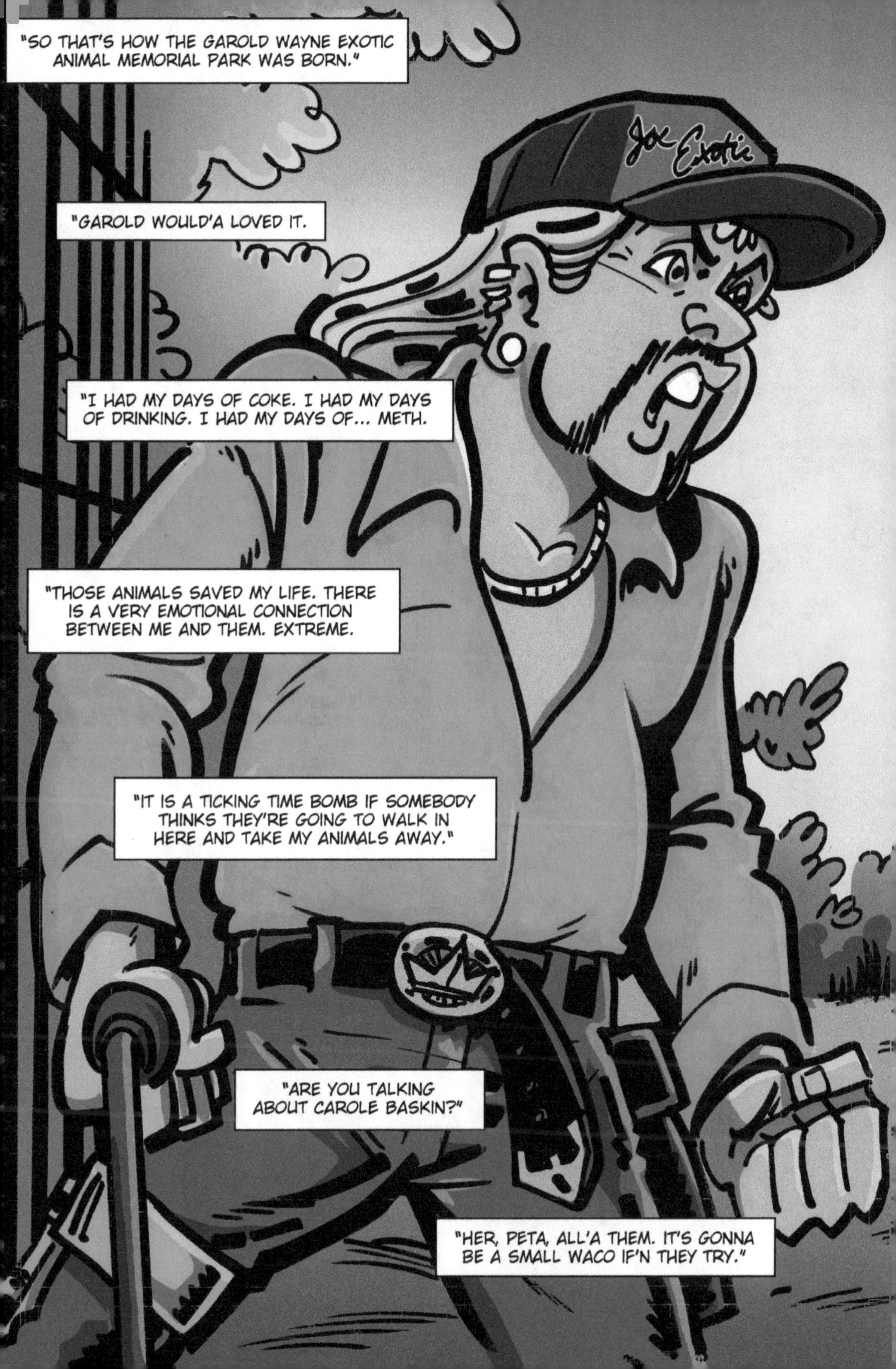
"SO THAT'S HOW THE GAROLD WAYNE EXOTIC ANIMAL MEMORIAL PARK WAS BORN."
Joe Exotic
"GAROLD WOULD'A LOVED IT.
"I HAD MY DAYS OF COKE. I HAD MY DAYS OF DRINKING. I HAD MY DAYS OF... METH.
"THOSE ANIMALS SAVED MY LIFE. THERE IS A VERY EMOTIONAL CONNECTION BETWEEN ME AND THEM. EXTREME.
"IT IS A TICKING TIME BOMB IF SOMEBODY THINKS THEY'RE GOING TO WALK IN HERE AND TAKE MY ANIMALS AWAY."
"ARE YOU TALKING ABOUT CAROLE BASKIN?"
"HER, PETA, ALL'A THEM. IT'S GONNA BE A SMALL WACO IF'N THEY TRY."

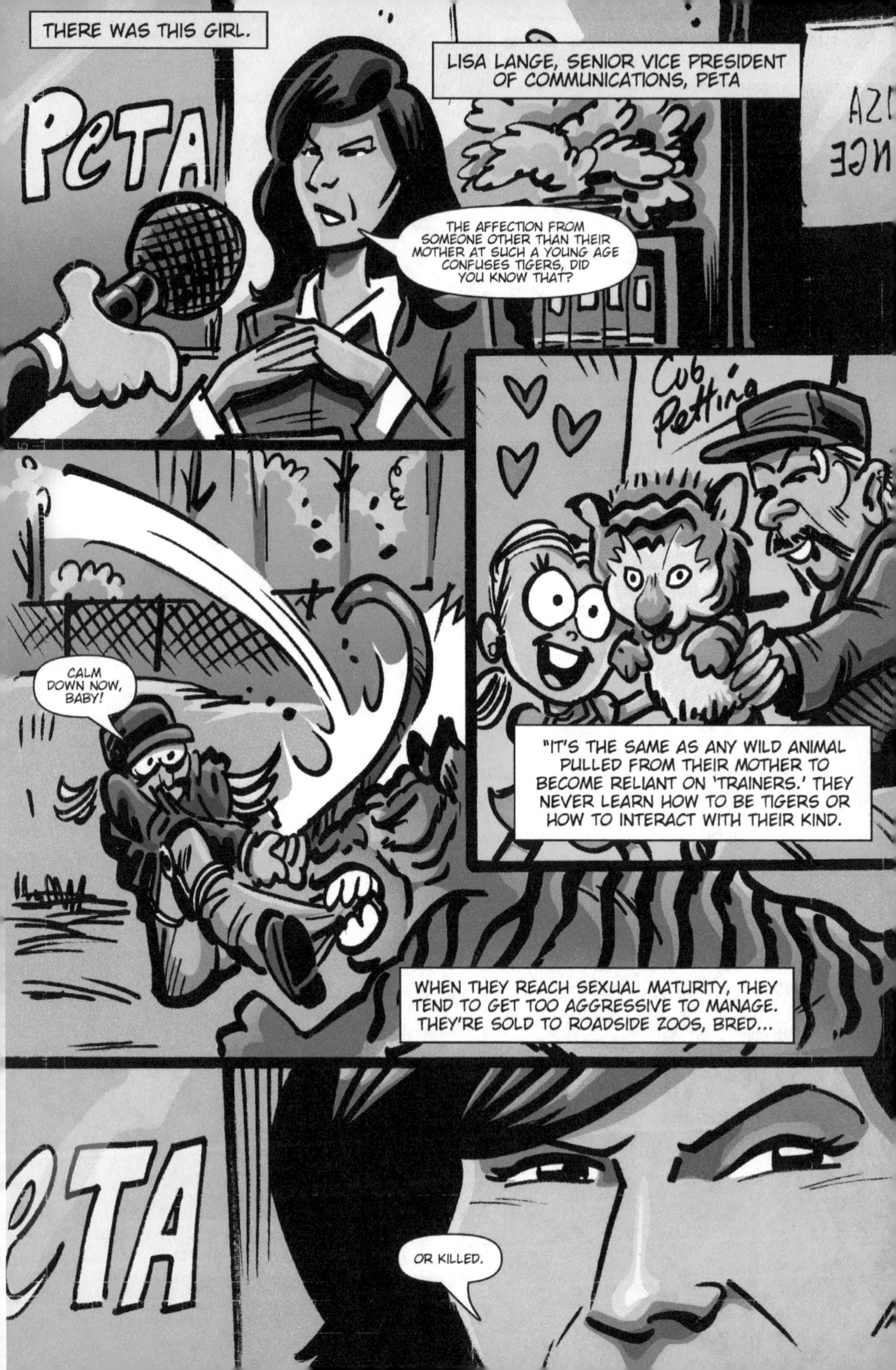
THERE WAS THIS GIRL.
LISA LANGE, SENIOR VICE PRESIDENT OF COMMUNICATIONS, PETA
PETA
THE AFFECTION FROM SOMEONE OTHER THAN THEIR MOTHER AT SUCH A YOUNG AGE CONFUSES TIGERS, DID YOU KNOW THAT?
Cub Petting
"IT'S THE SAME AS ANY WILD ANIMAL PULLED FROM THEIR MOTHER TO BECOME RELIANT ON 'TRAINERS.' THEY NEVER LEARN HOW TO BE TIGERS OR HOW TO INTERACT WITH THEIR KIND.
CALM DOWN NOW, BABY!
WHEN THEY REACH SEXUAL MATURITY, THEY TEND TO GET TOO AGGRESSIVE TO MANAGE. THEY'RE SOLD TO ROADSIDE ZOOS, BRED...
ETA
OR KILLED.

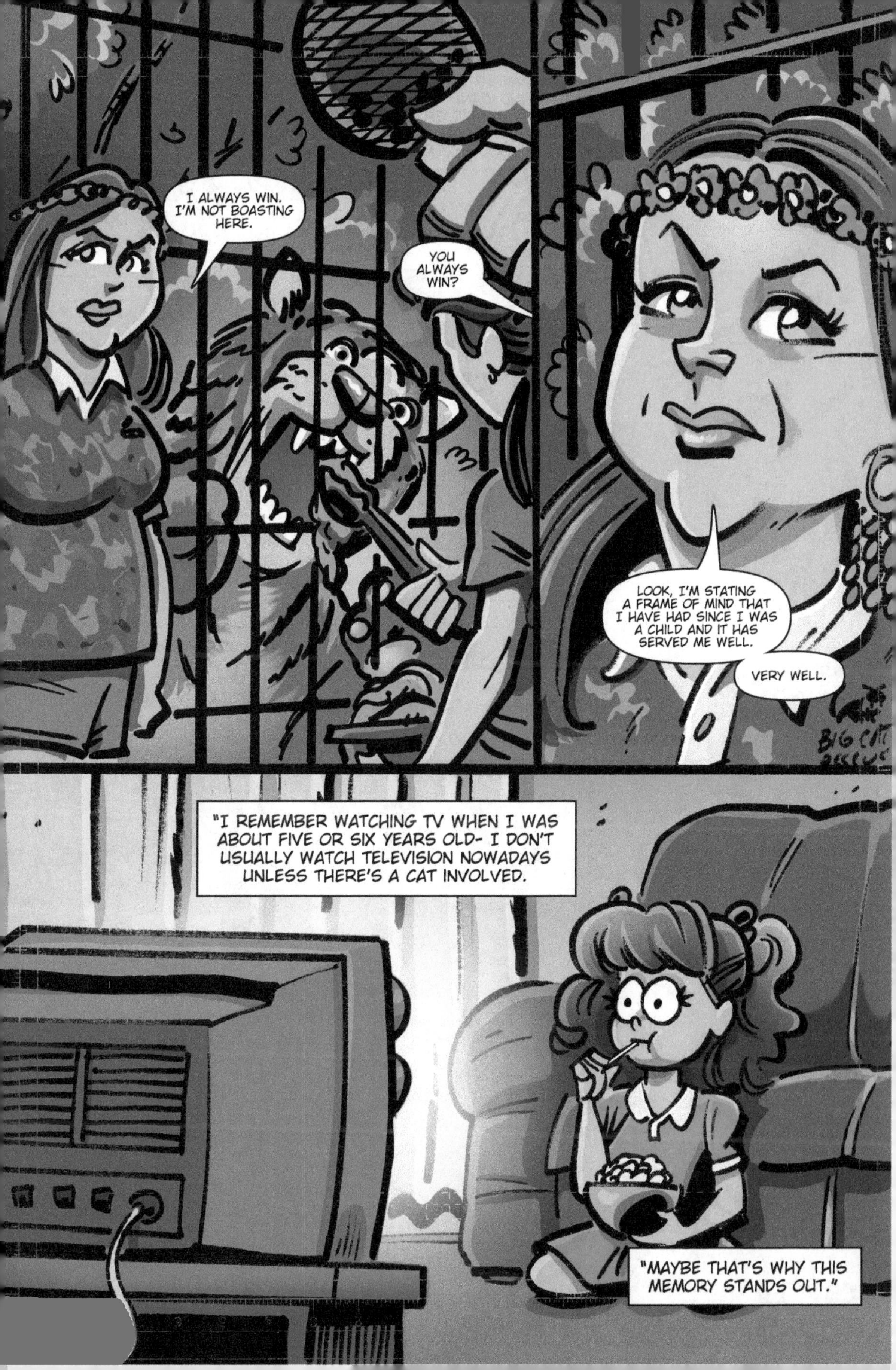
I ALWAYS WIN. I'M NOT BOASTING HERE.
YOU ALWAYS WIN?
LOOK, I'M STATING A FRAME OF MIND THAT I HAVE HAD SINCE I WAS A CHILD AND IT HAS SERVED ME WELL.
VERY WELL.
"I REMEMBER WATCHING TV WHEN I WAS ABOUT FIVE OR SIX YEARS OLD- I DON'T USUALLY WATCH TELEVISION NOWADAYS UNLESS THERE'S A CAT INVOLVED.
"MAYBE THAT'S WHY THIS MEMORY STANDS OUT."

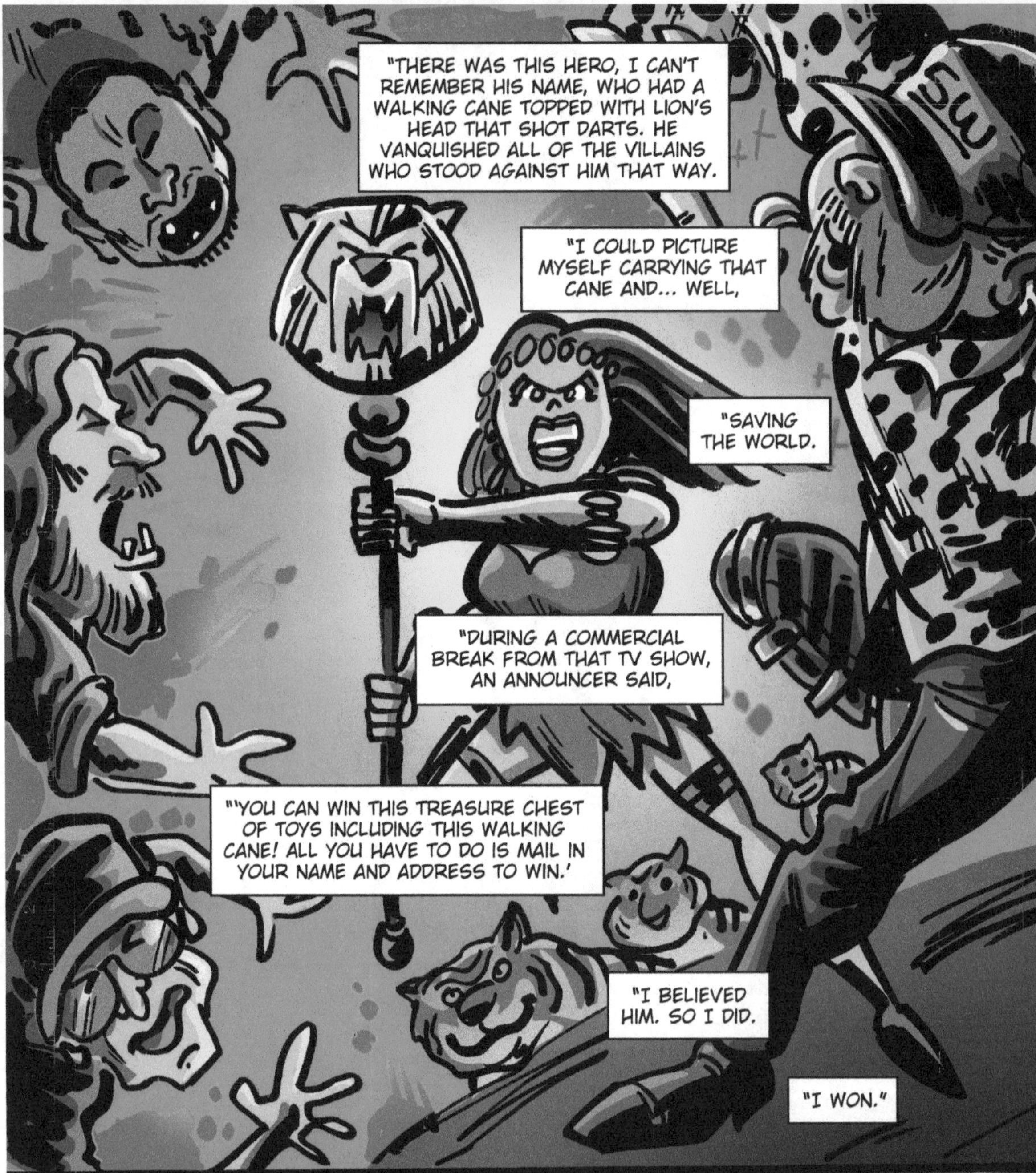
"THERE WAS THIS HERO, I CAN'T REMEMBER HIS NAME, WHO HAD A WALKING CANE TOPPED WITH LION'S HEAD THAT SHOT DARTS. HE VANQUISHED ALL OF THE VILLAINS WHO STOOD AGAINST HIM THAT WAY.
"I COULD PICTURE MYSELF CARRYING THAT CANE AND... WELL,
"SAVING THE WORLD.
"DURING A COMMERCIAL BREAK FROM THAT TV SHOW, AN ANNOUNCER SAID,
"'YOU CAN WIN THIS TREASURE CHEST OF TOYS INCLUDING THIS WALKING CANE! ALL YOU HAVE TO DO IS MAIL IN YOUR NAME AND ADDRESS TO WIN.'
"I BELIEVED HIM. SO I DID.
"I WON."
SW
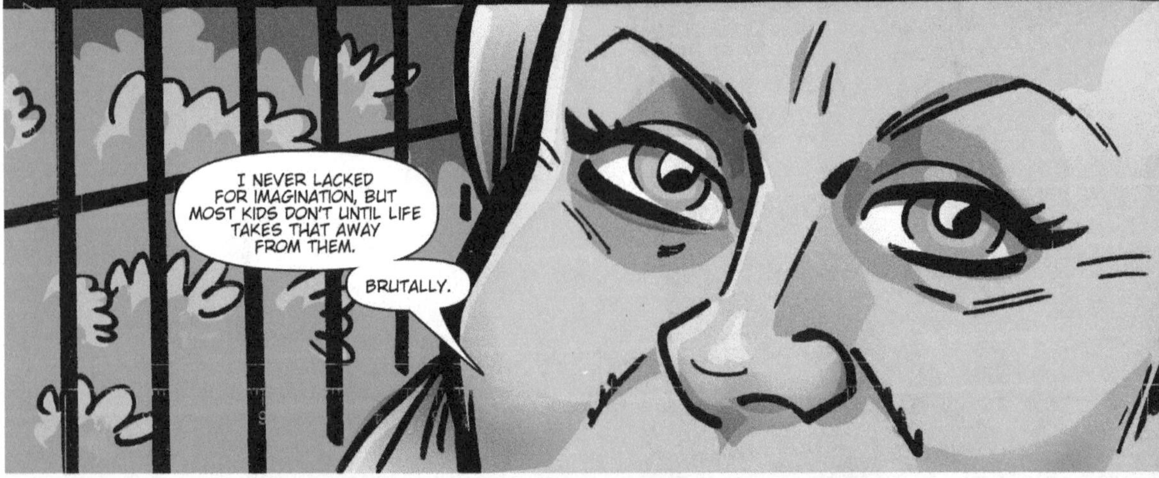
I NEVER LACKED FOR IMAGINATION, BUT MOST KIDS DON'T UNTIL LIFE TAKES THAT AWAY FROM THEM.
BRUTALLY.

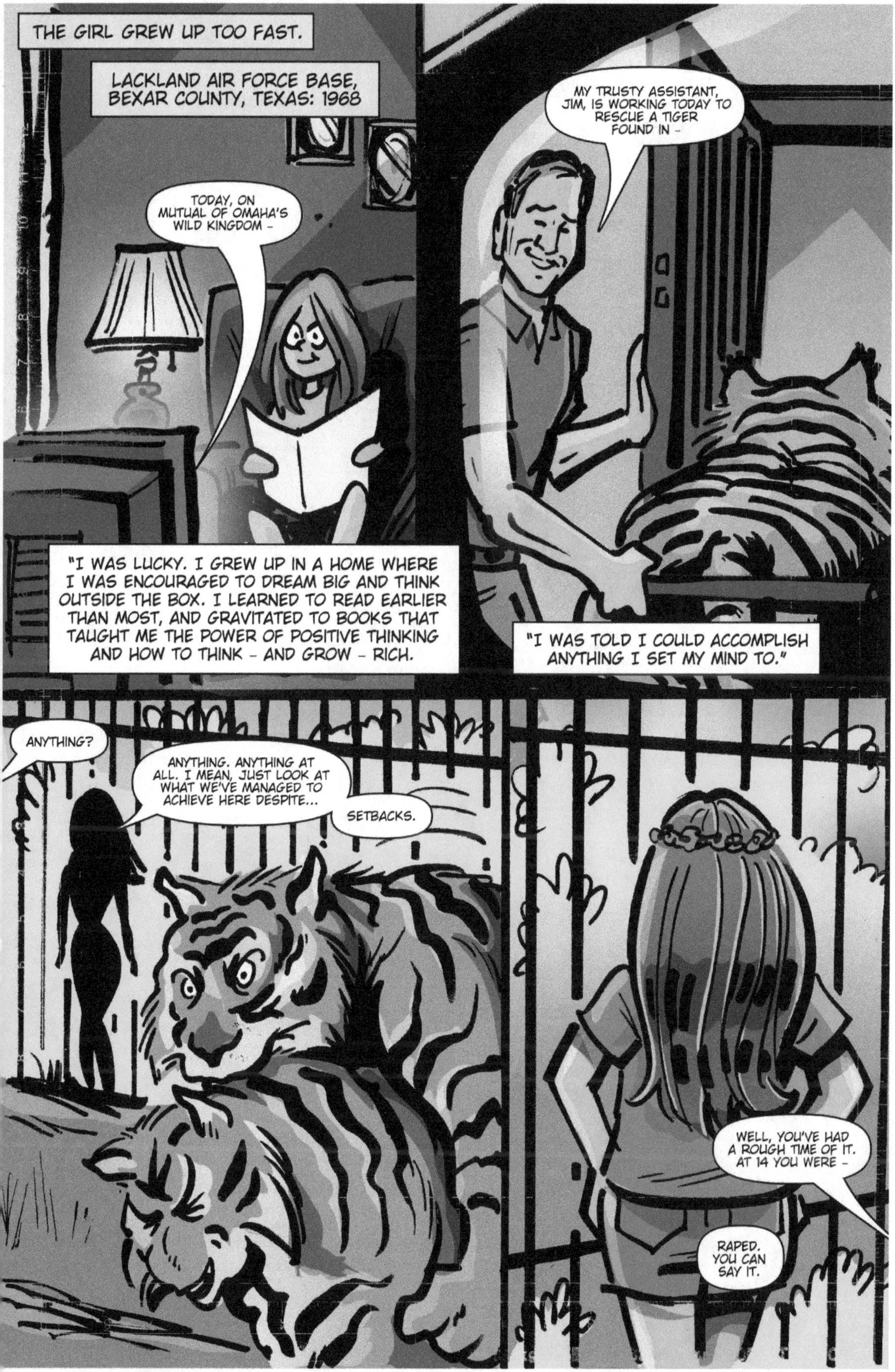
THE GIRL GREW UP TOO FAST.
LACKLAND AIR FORCE BASE, BEXAR COUNTY, TEXAS: 1968
TODAY, ON MUTUAL OF OMAHA'S WILD KINGDOM –
MY TRUSTY ASSISTANT, JIM, IS WORKING TODAY TO RESCUE A TIGER FOUND IN –
"I WAS LUCKY. I GREW UP IN A HOME WHERE I WAS ENCOURAGED TO DREAM BIG AND THINK OUTSIDE THE BOX. I LEARNED TO READ EARLIER THAN MOST, AND GRAVITATED TO BOOKS THAT TAUGHT ME THE POWER OF POSITIVE THINKING AND HOW TO THINK – AND GROW – RICH.
"I WAS TOLD I COULD ACCOMPLISH ANYTHING I SET MY MIND TO."
ANYTHING?
ANYTHING. ANYTHING AT ALL. I MEAN, JUST LOOK AT WHAT WE'VE MANAGED TO ACHIEVE HERE DESPITE...
SETBACKS.
WELL, YOU'VE HAD A ROUGH TIME OF IT. AT 14 YOU WERE –
RAPED. YOU CAN SAY IT.

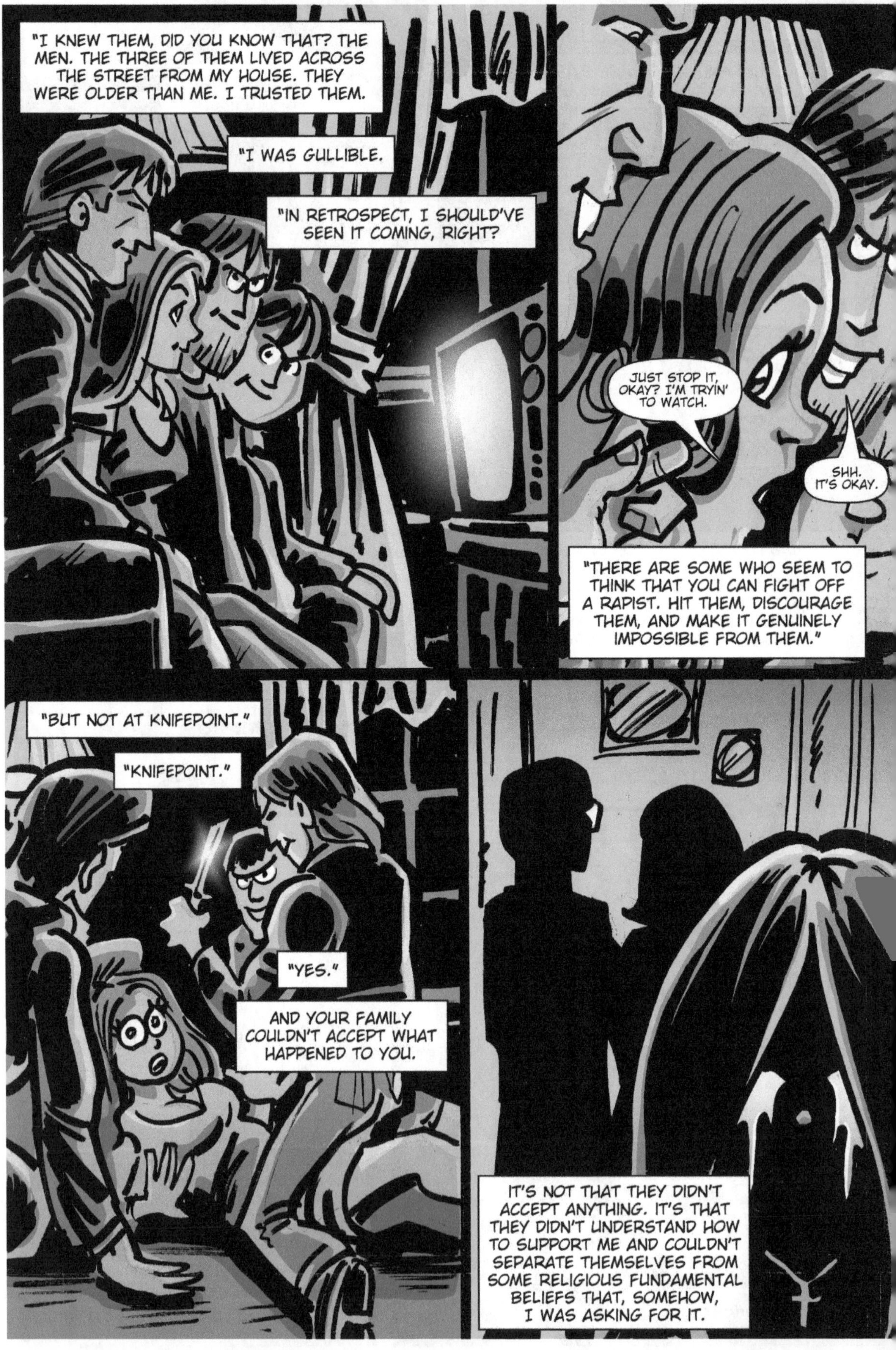

"I KNEW THEM, DID YOU KNOW THAT? THE MEN. THE THREE OF THEM LIVED ACROSS THE STREET FROM MY HOUSE. THEY WERE OLDER THAN ME. I TRUSTED THEM.
"I WAS GULLIBLE.
"IN RETROSPECT, I SHOULD'VE SEEN IT COMING, RIGHT?
JUST STOP IT, OKAY? I'M TRYIN' TO WATCH.
SHH. IT'S OKAY.
"THERE ARE SOME WHO SEEM TO THINK THAT YOU CAN FIGHT OFF A RAPIST. HIT THEM, DISCOURAGE THEM, AND MAKE IT GENUINELY IMPOSSIBLE FROM THEM."
"BUT NOT AT KNIFEPOINT."
"KNIFEPOINT."
"YES."
AND YOUR FAMILY COULDN'T ACCEPT WHAT HAPPENED TO YOU.
IT'S NOT THAT THEY DIDN'T ACCEPT ANYTHING. IT'S THAT THEY DIDN'T UNDERSTAND HOW TO SUPPORT ME AND COULDN'T SEPARATE THEMSELVES FROM SOME RELIGIOUS FUNDAMENTAL BELIEFS THAT, SOMEHOW, I WAS ASKING FOR IT.

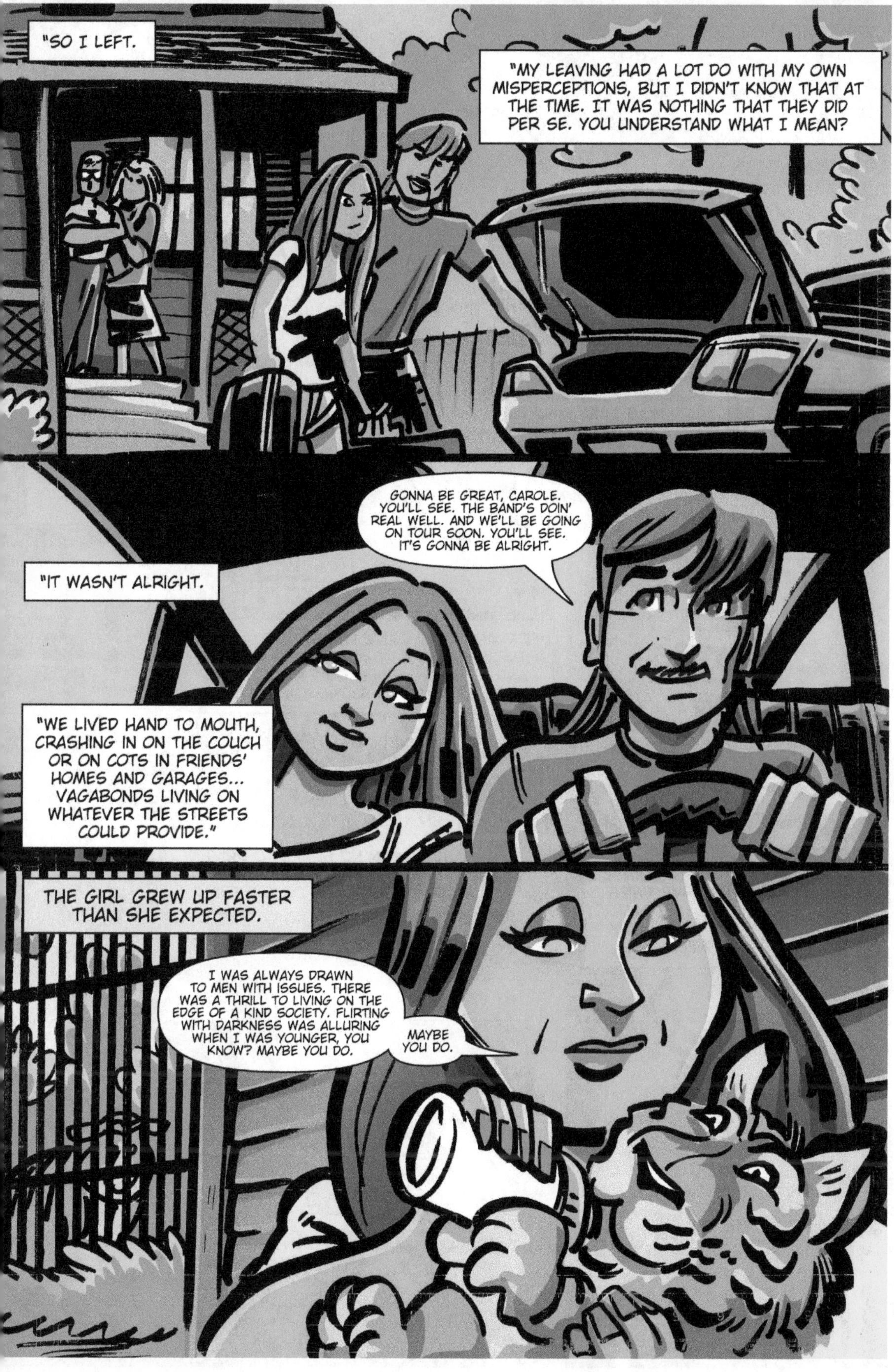
"SO I LEFT.
"MY LEAVING HAD A LOT DO WITH MY OWN MISPERCEPTIONS, BUT I DIDN'T KNOW THAT AT THE TIME. IT WAS NOTHING THAT THEY DID PER SE. YOU UNDERSTAND WHAT I MEAN?
GONNA BE GREAT, CAROLE. YOU'LL SEE. THE BAND'S DOIN' REAL WELL. AND WE'LL BE GOING ON TOUR SOON. YOU'LL SEE. IT'S GONNA BE ALRIGHT.
"IT WASN'T ALRIGHT.
"WE LIVED HAND TO MOUTH, CRASHING IN ON THE COUCH OR ON COTS IN FRIENDS' HOMES AND GARAGES... VAGABONDS LIVING ON WHATEVER THE STREETS COULD PROVIDE."
THE GIRL GREW UP FASTER THAN SHE EXPECTED.
I WAS ALWAYS DRAWN TO MEN WITH ISSUES. THERE WAS A THRILL TO LIVING ON THE EDGE OF A KIND SOCIETY. FLIRTING WITH DARKNESS WAS ALLURING WHEN I WAS YOUNGER, YOU KNOW? MAYBE YOU DO.
MAYBE YOU DO.

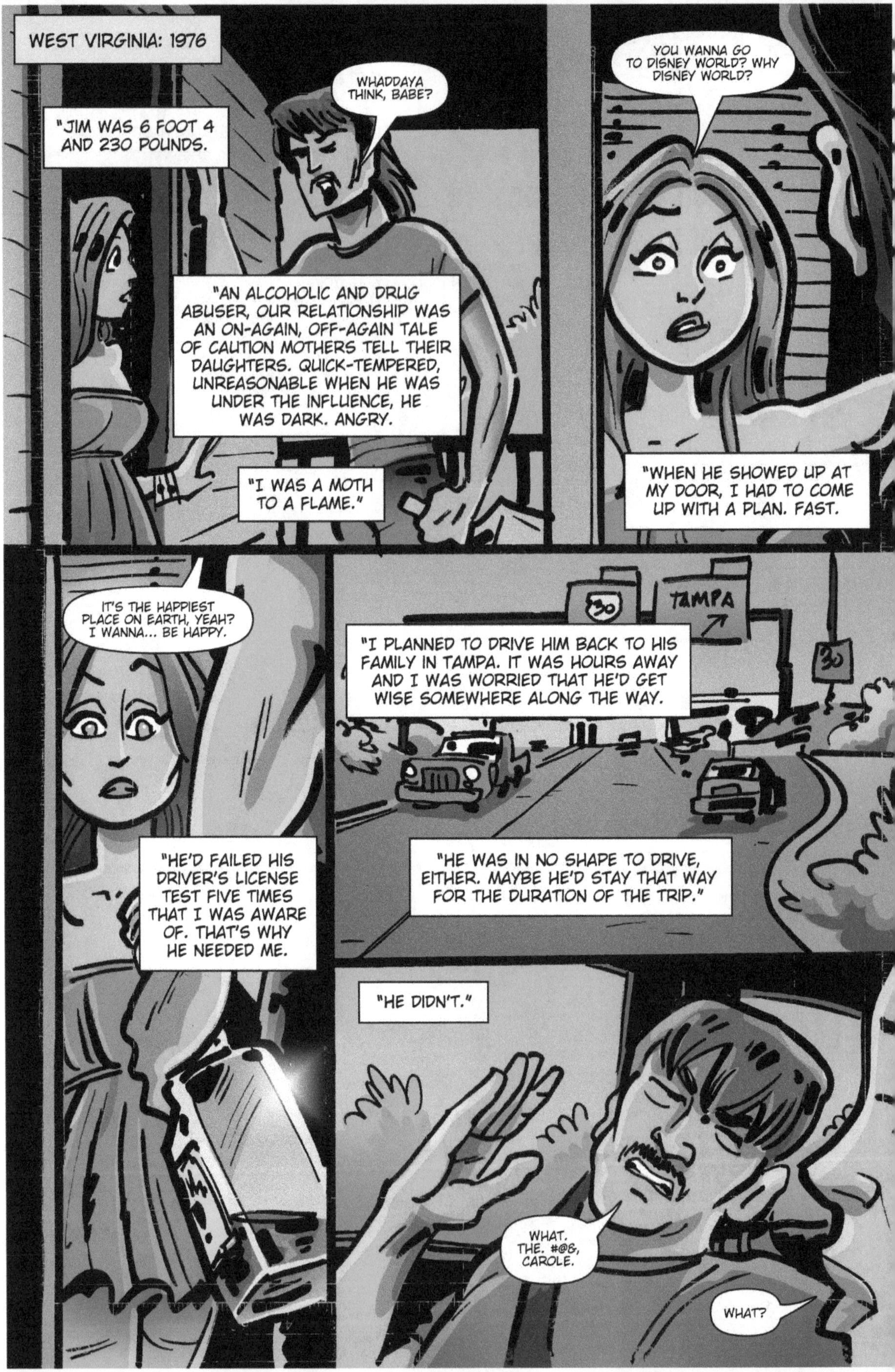
WEST VIRGINIA: 1976
"JIM WAS 6 FOOT 4 AND 230 POUNDS.
WHADDAYA THINK, BABE?
"AN ALCOHOLIC AND DRUG ABUSER, OUR RELATIONSHIP WAS AN ON-AGAIN, OFF-AGAIN TALE OF CAUTION MOTHERS TELL THEIR DAUGHTERS. QUICK-TEMPERED, UNREASONABLE WHEN HE WAS UNDER THE INFLUENCE, HE WAS DARK. ANGRY.
"I WAS A MOTH TO A FLAME."
YOU WANNA GO TO DISNEY WORLD? WHY DISNEY WORLD?
"WHEN HE SHOWED UP AT MY DOOR, I HAD TO COME UP WITH A PLAN. FAST.
IT'S THE HAPPIEST PLACE ON EARTH, YEAH? I WANNA... BE HAPPY.
"HE'D FAILED HIS DRIVER'S LICENSE TEST FIVE TIMES THAT I WAS AWARE OF. THAT'S WHY HE NEEDED ME.
30
TAMPA
"I PLANNED TO DRIVE HIM BACK TO HIS FAMILY IN TAMPA. IT WAS HOURS AWAY AND I WAS WORRIED THAT HE'D GET WISE SOMEWHERE ALONG THE WAY.
30
"HE WAS IN NO SHAPE TO DRIVE, EITHER. MAYBE HE'D STAY THAT WAY FOR THE DURATION OF THE TRIP."
"HE DIDN'T."
WHAT. THE. #@&, CAROLE.
WHAT?

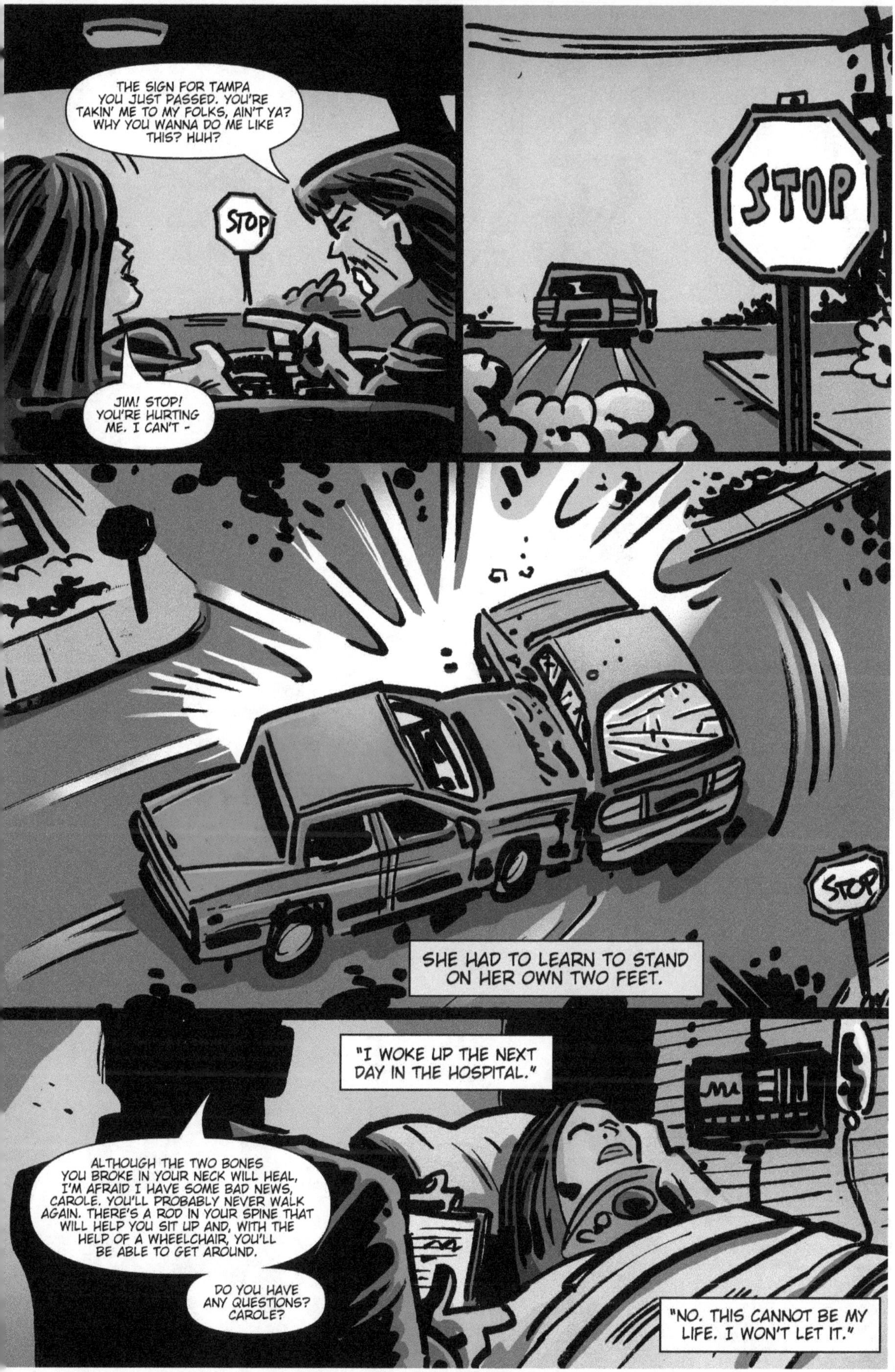
THE SIGN FOR TAMPA YOU JUST PASSED. YOU'RE TAKIN' ME TO MY FOLKS, AIN'T YA? WHY YOU WANNA DO ME LIKE THIS? HUH?
STOP
JIM! STOP! YOU'RE HURTING ME. I CAN'T -
STOP
STOP
SHE HAD TO LEARN TO STAND ON HER OWN TWO FEET.
"I WOKE UP THE NEXT DAY IN THE HOSPITAL."
ALTHOUGH THE TWO BONES YOU BROKE IN YOUR NECK WILL HEAL, I'M AFRAID I HAVE SOME BAD NEWS, CAROLE. YOU'LL PROBABLY NEVER WALK AGAIN. THERE'S A ROD IN YOUR SPINE THAT WILL HELP YOU SIT UP AND, WITH THE HELP OF A WHEELCHAIR, YOU'LL BE ABLE TO GET AROUND.
DO YOU HAVE ANY QUESTIONS? CAROLE?
"NO. THIS CANNOT BE MY LIFE. I WON'T LET IT."

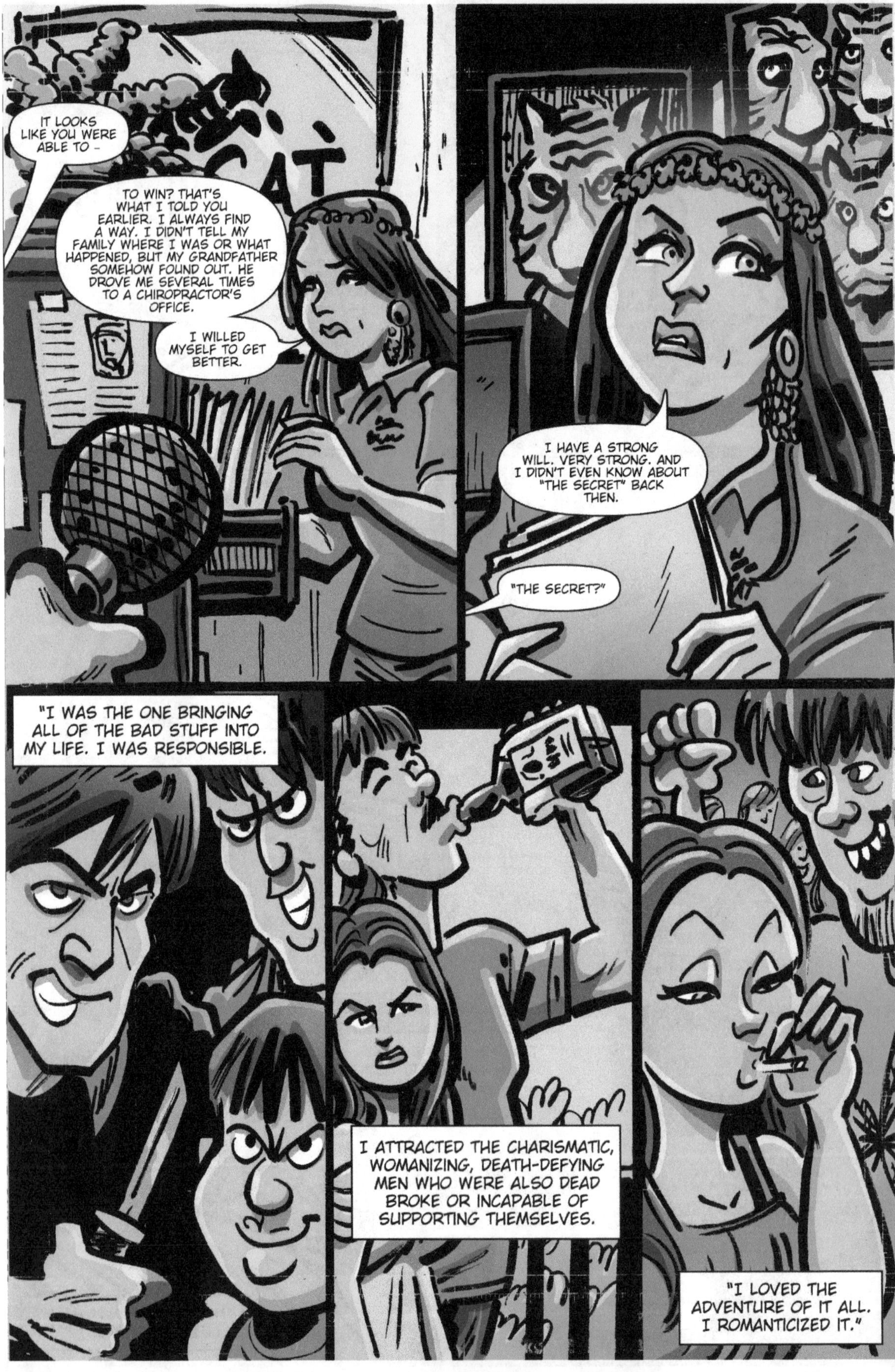

IT LOOKS LIKE YOU WERE ABLE TO –
TO WIN? THAT'S WHAT I TOLD YOU EARLIER. I ALWAYS FIND A WAY. I DIDN'T TELL MY FAMILY WHERE I WAS OR WHAT HAPPENED, BUT MY GRANDFATHER SOMEHOW FOUND OUT. HE DROVE ME SEVERAL TIMES TO A CHIROPRACTOR'S OFFICE.
I WILLED MYSELF TO GET BETTER.
CAT
I HAVE A STRONG WILL. VERY STRONG. AND I DIDN'T EVEN KNOW ABOUT "THE SECRET" BACK THEN.
"THE SECRET?"
"I WAS THE ONE BRINGING ALL OF THE BAD STUFF INTO MY LIFE. I WAS RESPONSIBLE.
I ATTRACTED THE CHARISMATIC, WOMANIZING, DEATH-DEFYING MEN WHO WERE ALSO DEAD BROKE OR INCAPABLE OF SUPPORTING THEMSELVES.
"I LOVED THE ADVENTURE OF IT ALL. I ROMANTICIZED IT."

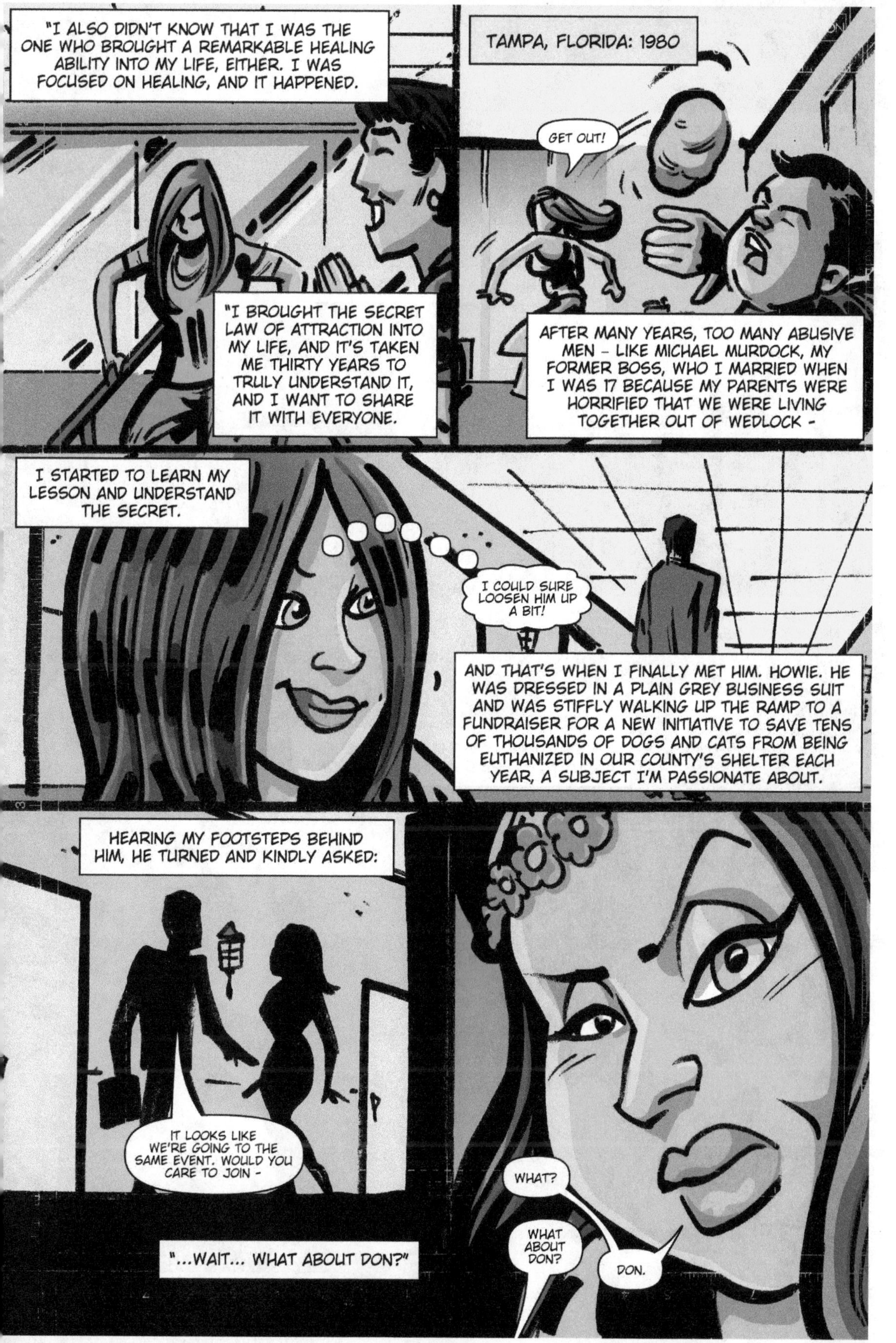
"I ALSO DIDN'T KNOW THAT I WAS THE ONE WHO BROUGHT A REMARKABLE HEALING ABILITY INTO MY LIFE, EITHER. I WAS FOCUSED ON HEALING, AND IT HAPPENED.
"I BROUGHT THE SECRET LAW OF ATTRACTION INTO MY LIFE, AND IT'S TAKEN ME THIRTY YEARS TO TRULY UNDERSTAND IT, AND I WANT TO SHARE IT WITH EVERYONE.
TAMPA, FLORIDA: 1980
GET OUT!
AFTER MANY YEARS, TOO MANY ABUSIVE MEN – LIKE MICHAEL MURDOCK, MY FORMER BOSS, WHO I MARRIED WHEN I WAS 17 BECAUSE MY PARENTS WERE HORRIFIED THAT WE WERE LIVING TOGETHER OUT OF WEDLOCK –
I STARTED TO LEARN MY LESSON AND UNDERSTAND THE SECRET.
I COULD SURE LOOSEN HIM UP A BIT!
AND THAT'S WHEN I FINALLY MET HIM. HOWIE. HE WAS DRESSED IN A PLAIN GREY BUSINESS SUIT AND WAS STIFFLY WALKING UP THE RAMP TO A FUNDRAISER FOR A NEW INITIATIVE TO SAVE TENS OF THOUSANDS OF DOGS AND CATS FROM BEING EUTHANIZED IN OUR COUNTY'S SHELTER EACH YEAR, A SUBJECT I'M PASSIONATE ABOUT.
HEARING MY FOOTSTEPS BEHIND HIM, HE TURNED AND KINDLY ASKED:
IT LOOKS LIKE WE'RE GOING TO THE SAME EVENT. WOULD YOU CARE TO JOIN –
"...WAIT... WHAT ABOUT DON?"
WHAT?
WHAT ABOUT DON?
DON.

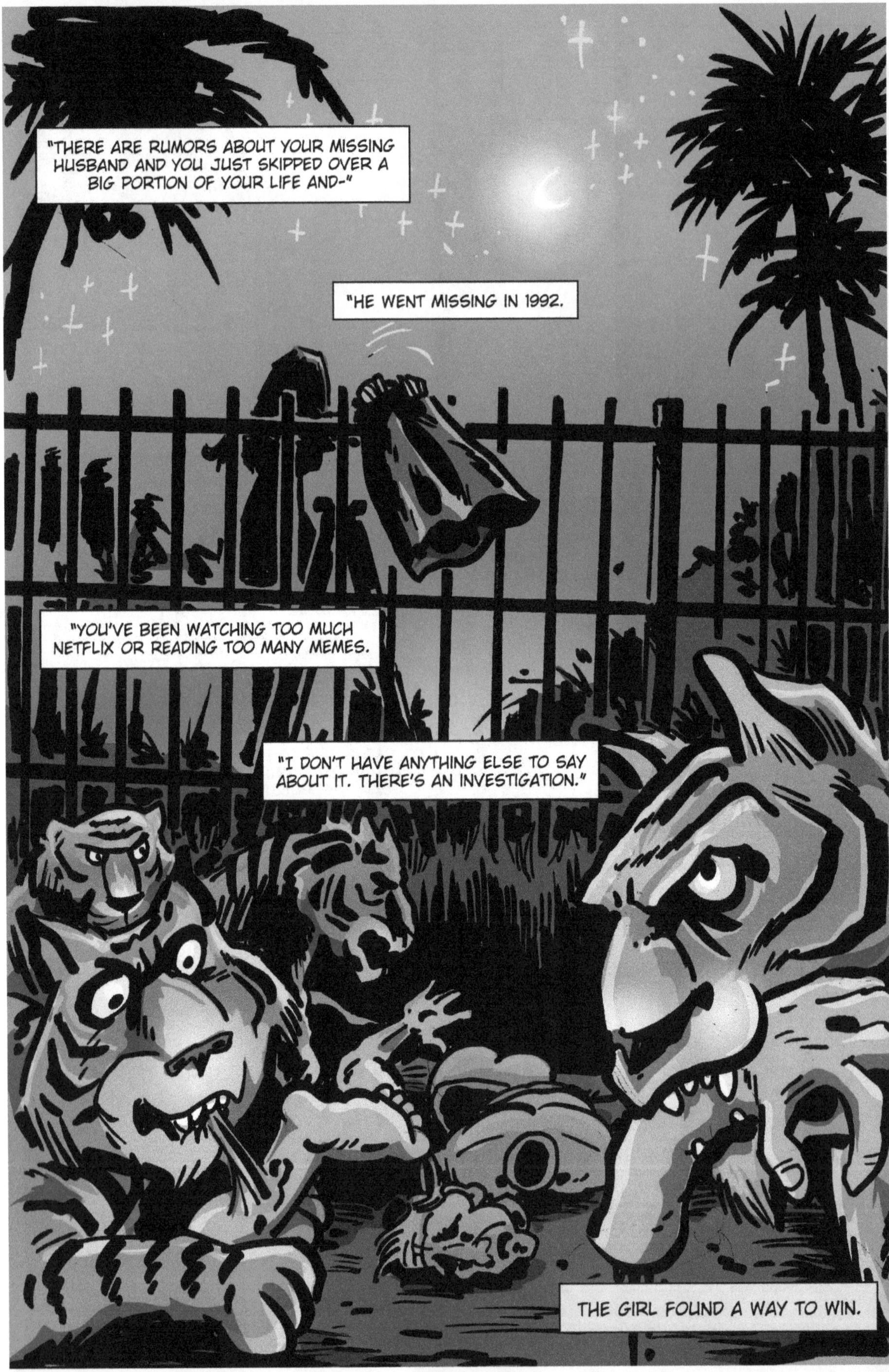
"THERE ARE RUMORS ABOUT YOUR MISSING HUSBAND AND YOU JUST SKIPPED OVER A BIG PORTION OF YOUR LIFE AND-"
"HE WENT MISSING IN 1992.
"YOU'VE BEEN WATCHING TOO MUCH NETFLIX OR READING TOO MANY MEMES.
"I DON'T HAVE ANYTHING ELSE TO SAY ABOUT IT. THERE'S AN INVESTIGATION."
THE GIRL FOUND A WAY TO WIN.

CHAPTER 2

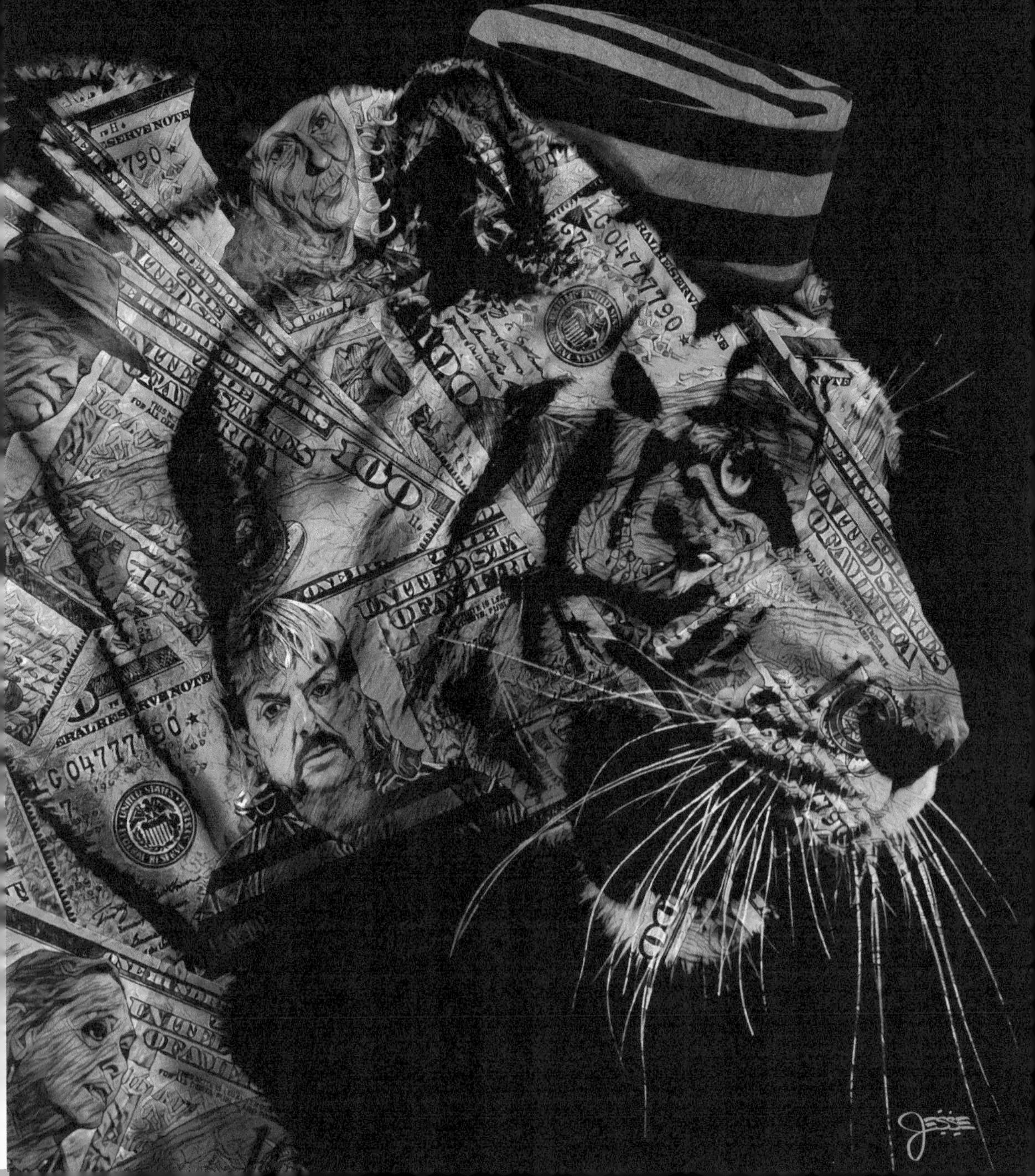

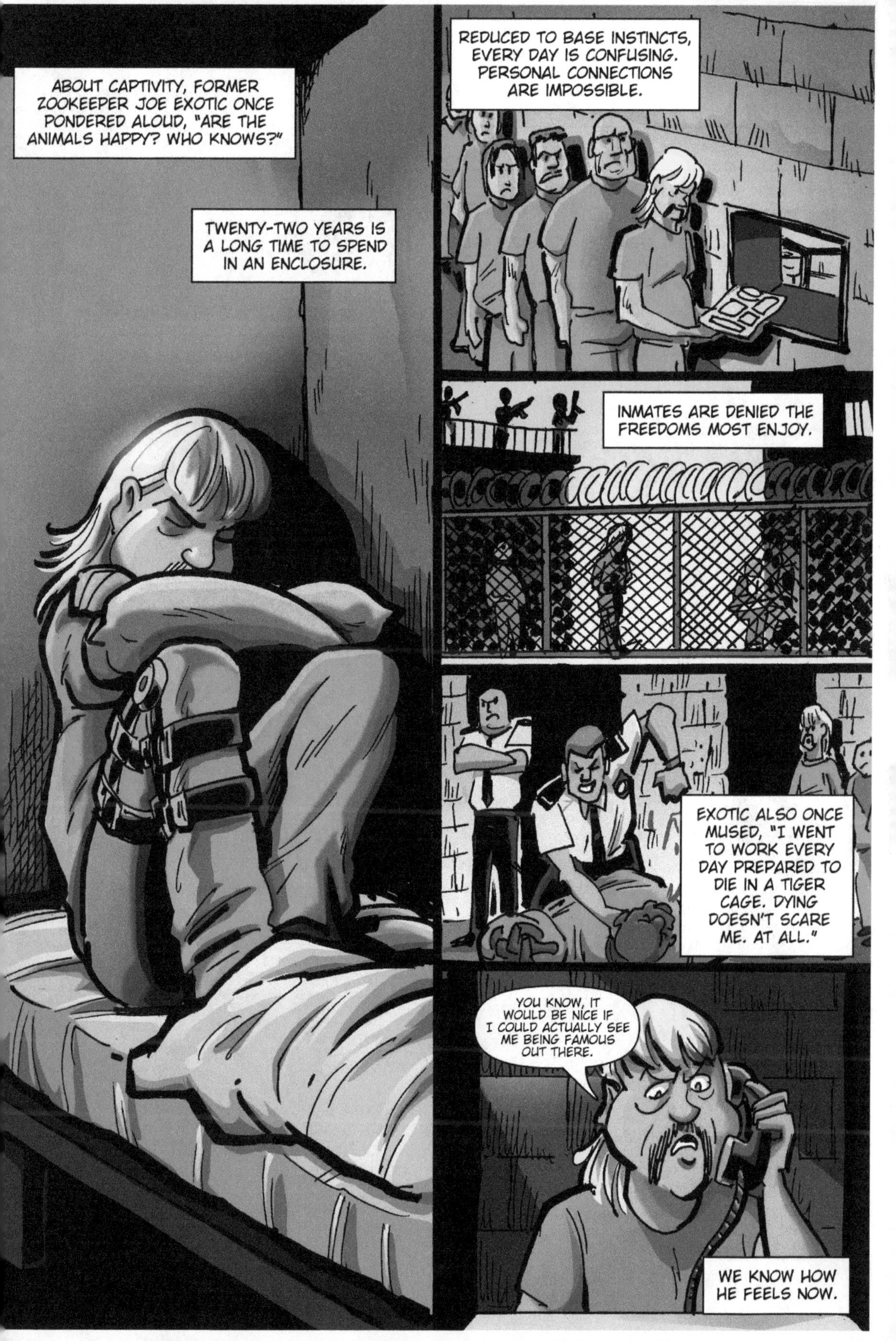

ABOUT CAPTIVITY, FORMER ZOOKEEPER JOE EXOTIC ONCE PONDERED ALOUD, "ARE THE ANIMALS HAPPY? WHO KNOWS?"
TWENTY-TWO YEARS IS A LONG TIME TO SPEND IN AN ENCLOSURE.
REDUCED TO BASE INSTINCTS, EVERY DAY IS CONFUSING. PERSONAL CONNECTIONS ARE IMPOSSIBLE.
INMATES ARE DENIED THE FREEDOMS MOST ENJOY.
EXOTIC ALSO ONCE MUSED, "I WENT TO WORK EVERY DAY PREPARED TO DIE IN A TIGER CAGE. DYING DOESN'T SCARE ME. AT ALL."
YOU KNOW, IT WOULD BE NICE IF I COULD ACTUALLY SEE ME BEING FAMOUS OUT THERE.
WE KNOW HOW HE FEELS NOW.

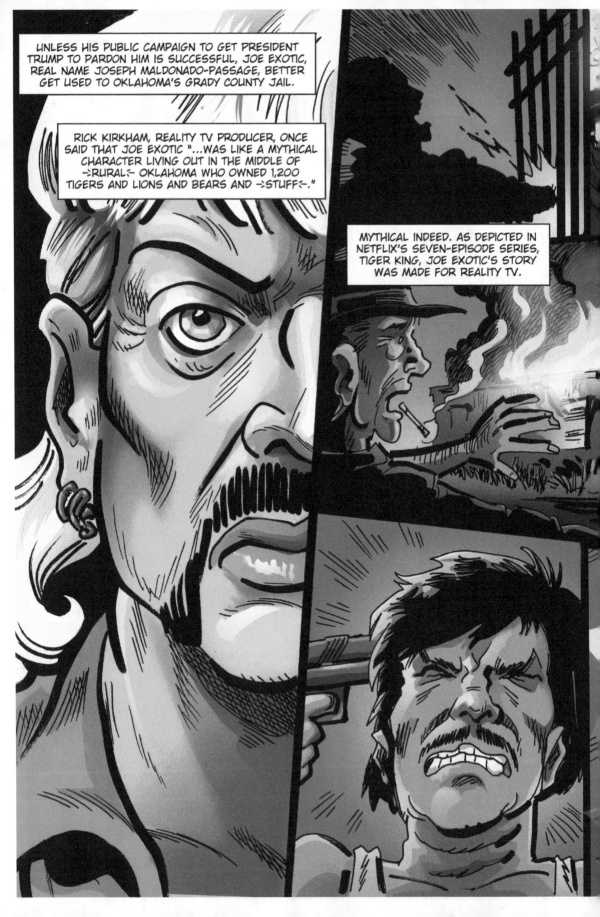

UNLESS HIS PUBLIC CAMPAIGN TO GET PRESIDENT TRUMP TO PARDON HIM IS SUCCESSFUL, JOE EXOTIC, REAL NAME JOSEPH MALDONADO-PASSAGE, BETTER GET USED TO OKLAHOMA'S GRADY COUNTY JAIL.

RICK KIRKHAM, REALITY TV PRODUCER, ONCE SAID THAT JOE EXOTIC "...WAS LIKE A MYTHICAL CHARACTER LIVING OUT IN THE MIDDLE OF ⇥RURAL⇤ OKLAHOMA WHO OWNED 1,200 TIGERS AND LIONS AND BEARS AND ⇥STUFF⇤."

MYTHICAL INDEED. AS DEPICTED IN NETFLIX'S SEVEN-EPISODE SERIES, TIGER KING, JOE EXOTIC'S STORY WAS MADE FOR REALITY TV.

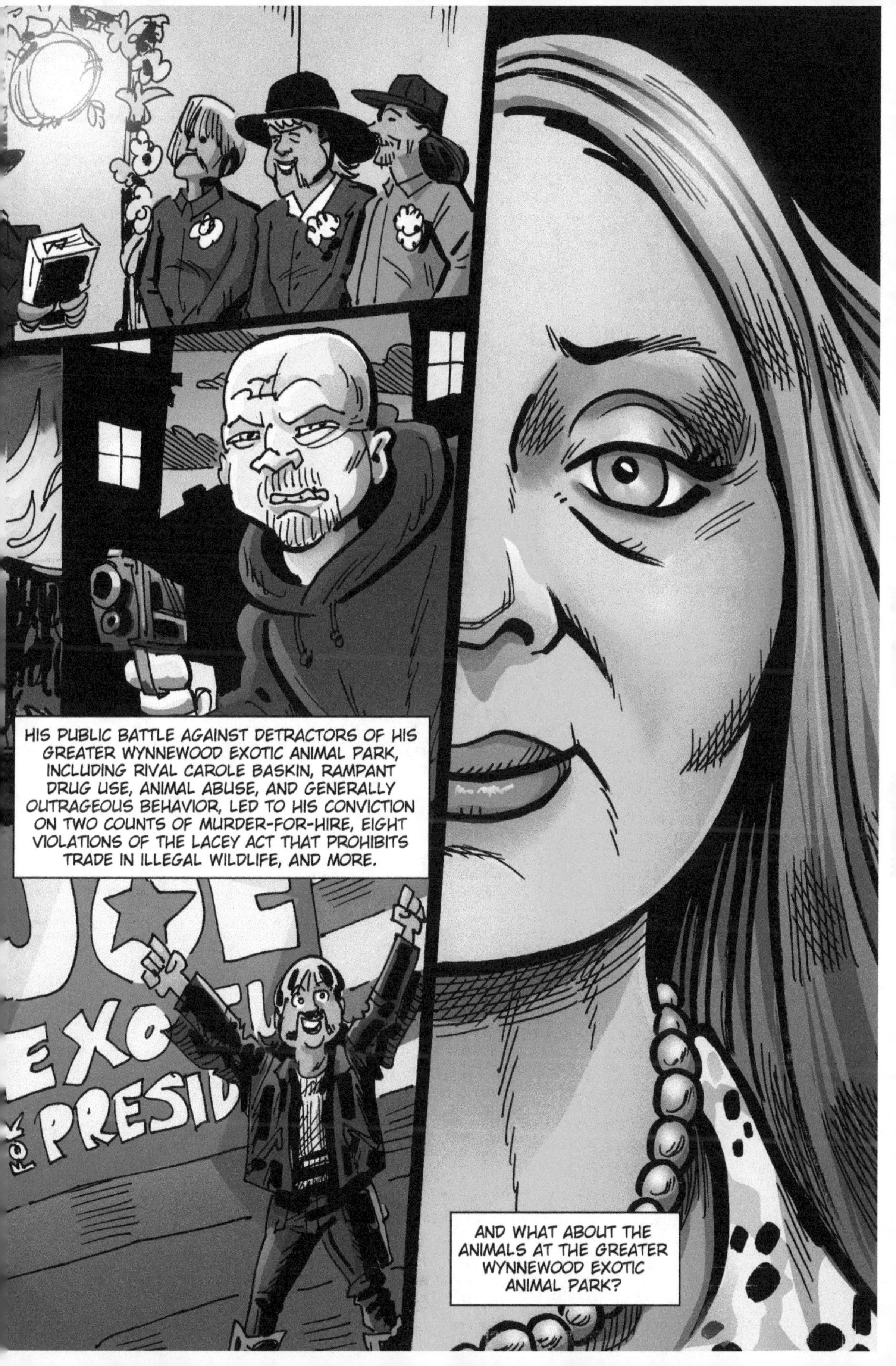
HIS PUBLIC BATTLE AGAINST DETRACTORS OF HIS GREATER WYNNEWOOD EXOTIC ANIMAL PARK, INCLUDING RIVAL CAROLE BASKIN, RAMPANT DRUG USE, ANIMAL ABUSE, AND GENERALLY OUTRAGEOUS BEHAVIOR, LED TO HIS CONVICTION ON TWO COUNTS OF MURDER-FOR-HIRE, EIGHT VIOLATIONS OF THE LACEY ACT THAT PROHIBITS TRADE IN ILLEGAL WILDLIFE, AND MORE.
EXO
FOR PRESID
AND WHAT ABOUT THE ANIMALS AT THE GREATER WYNNEWOOD EXOTIC ANIMAL PARK?

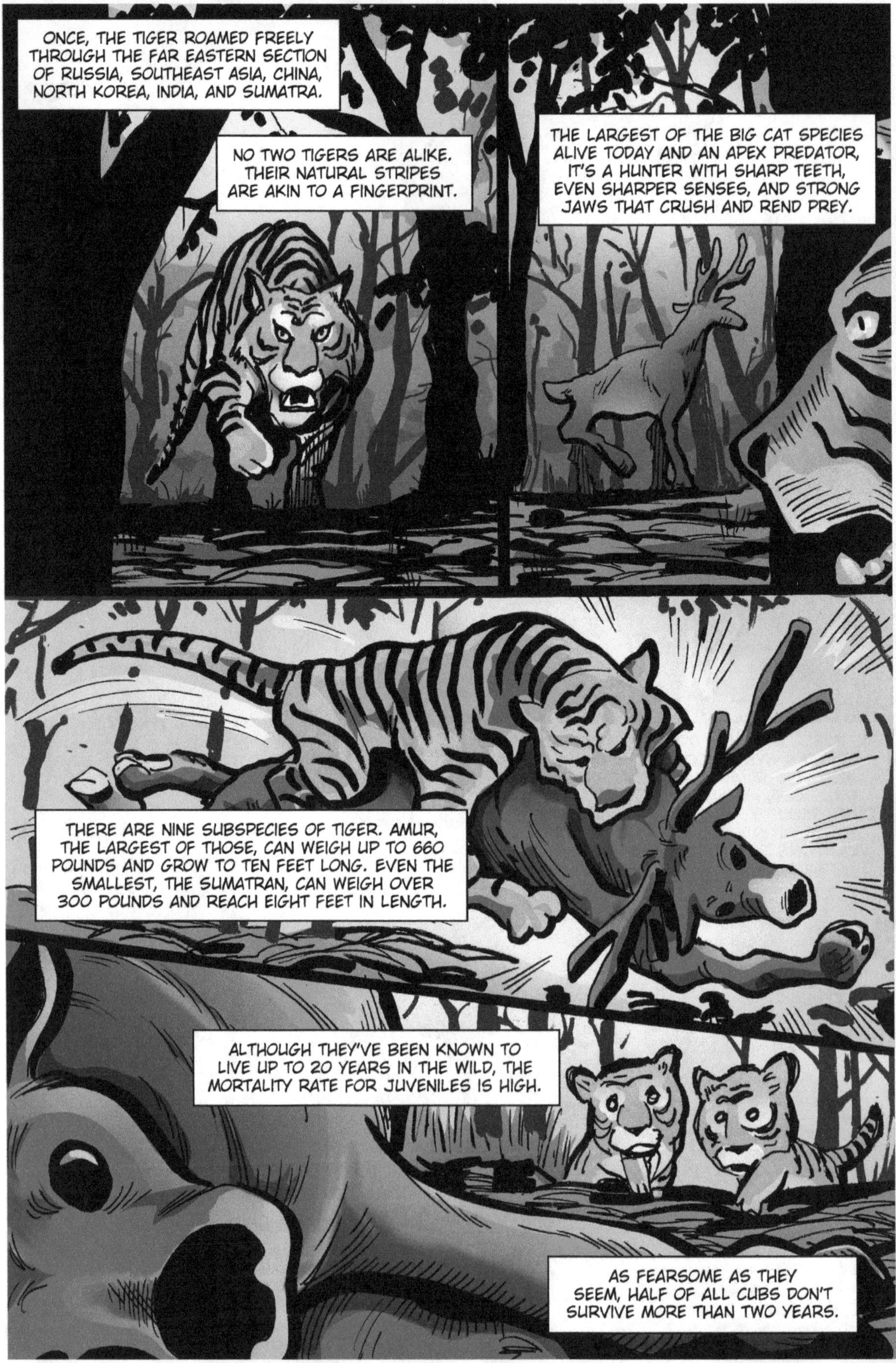
ONCE, THE TIGER ROAMED FREELY THROUGH THE FAR EASTERN SECTION OF RUSSIA, SOUTHEAST ASIA, CHINA, NORTH KOREA, INDIA, AND SUMATRA.
NO TWO TIGERS ARE ALIKE. THEIR NATURAL STRIPES ARE AKIN TO A FINGERPRINT.
THE LARGEST OF THE BIG CAT SPECIES ALIVE TODAY AND AN APEX PREDATOR, IT'S A HUNTER WITH SHARP TEETH, EVEN SHARPER SENSES, AND STRONG JAWS THAT CRUSH AND REND PREY.
THERE ARE NINE SUBSPECIES OF TIGER. AMUR, THE LARGEST OF THOSE, CAN WEIGH UP TO 660 POUNDS AND GROW TO TEN FEET LONG. EVEN THE SMALLEST, THE SUMATRAN, CAN WEIGH OVER 300 POUNDS AND REACH EIGHT FEET IN LENGTH.
ALTHOUGH THEY'VE BEEN KNOWN TO LIVE UP TO 20 YEARS IN THE WILD, THE MORTALITY RATE FOR JUVENILES IS HIGH.
AS FEARSOME AS THEY SEEM, HALF OF ALL CUBS DON'T SURVIVE MORE THAN TWO YEARS.

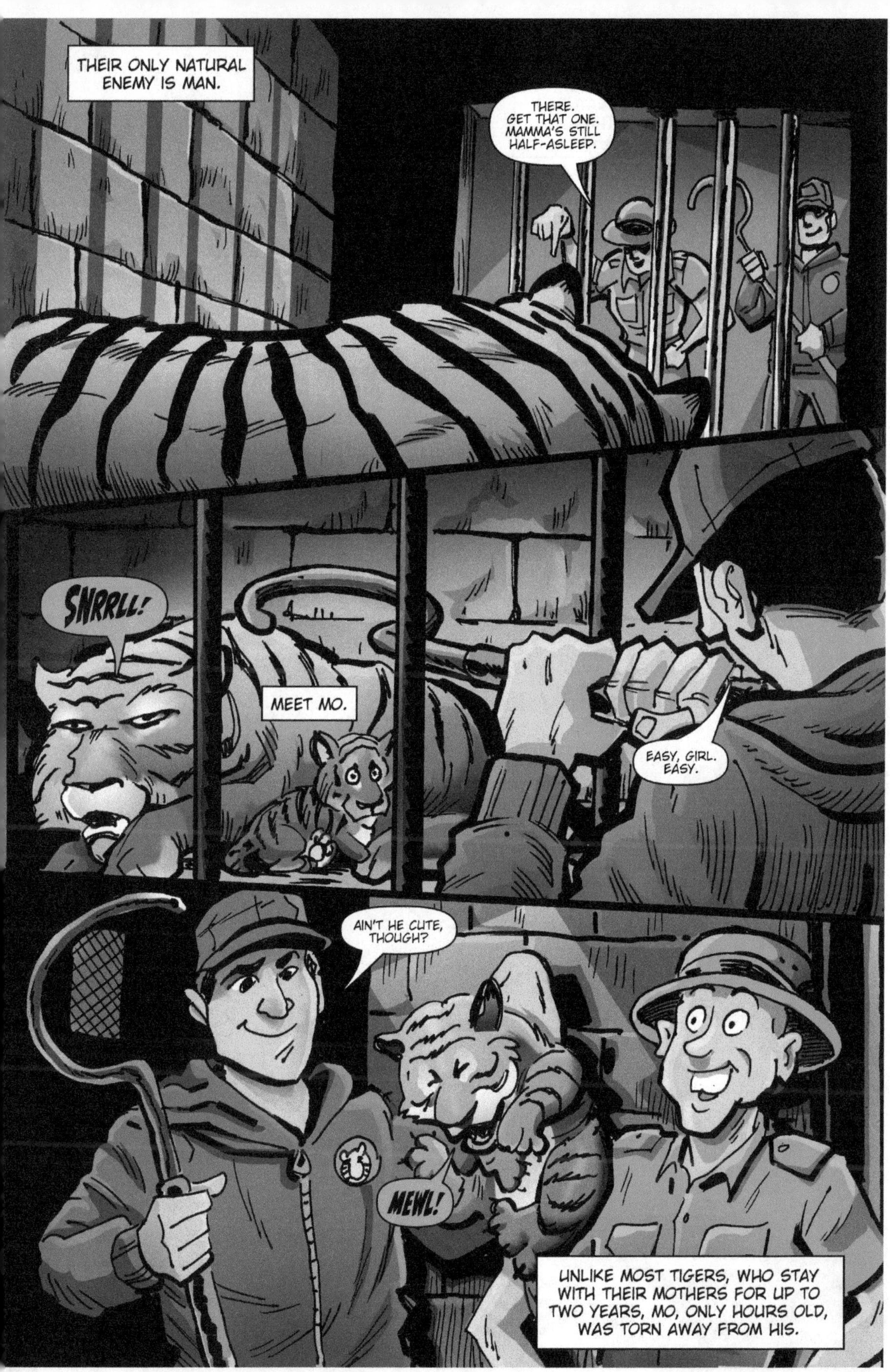
THEIR ONLY NATURAL ENEMY IS MAN.
THERE. GET THAT ONE. MAMMA'S STILL HALF-ASLEEP.
SNRRLL!
MEET MO.
EASY, GIRL. EASY.
AIN'T HE CUTE, THOUGH?
MEWL!
UNLIKE MOST TIGERS, WHO STAY WITH THEIR MOTHERS FOR UP TO TWO YEARS, MO, ONLY HOURS OLD, WAS TORN AWAY FROM HIS.

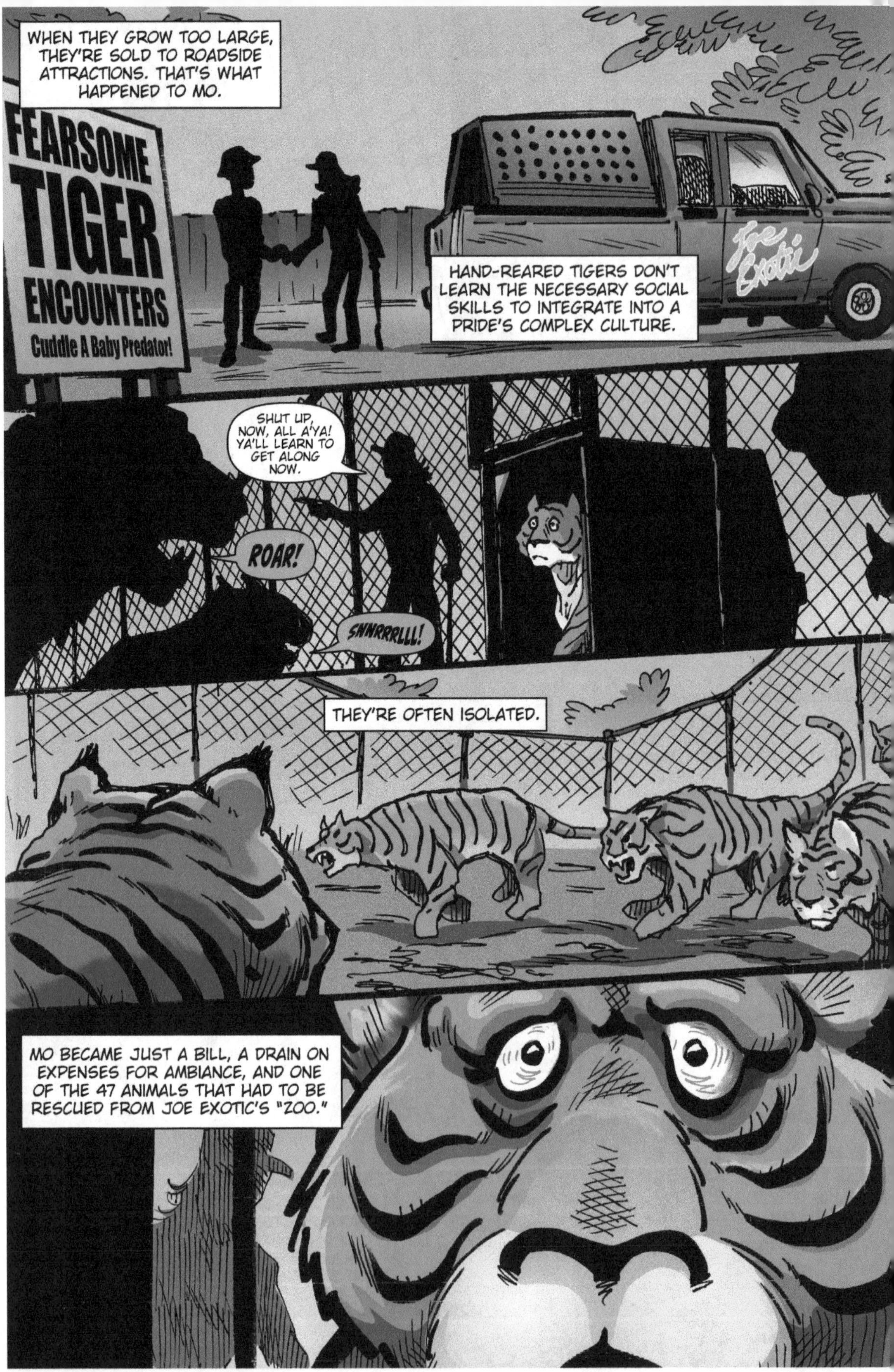

WHEN THEY GROW TOO LARGE, THEY'RE SOLD TO ROADSIDE ATTRACTIONS. THAT'S WHAT HAPPENED TO MO.
FEARSOME TIGER ENCOUNTERS
Cuddle A Baby Predator!
Joe Exotic
HAND-REARED TIGERS DON'T LEARN THE NECESSARY SOCIAL SKILLS TO INTEGRATE INTO A PRIDE'S COMPLEX CULTURE.
SHUT UP, NOW, ALL A'YA! YA'LL LEARN TO GET ALONG NOW.
ROAR!
SNNRRRLLL!
THEY'RE OFTEN ISOLATED.
MO BECAME JUST A BILL, A DRAIN ON EXPENSES FOR AMBIANCE, AND ONE OF THE 47 ANIMALS THAT HAD TO BE RESCUED FROM JOE EXOTIC'S "ZOO."

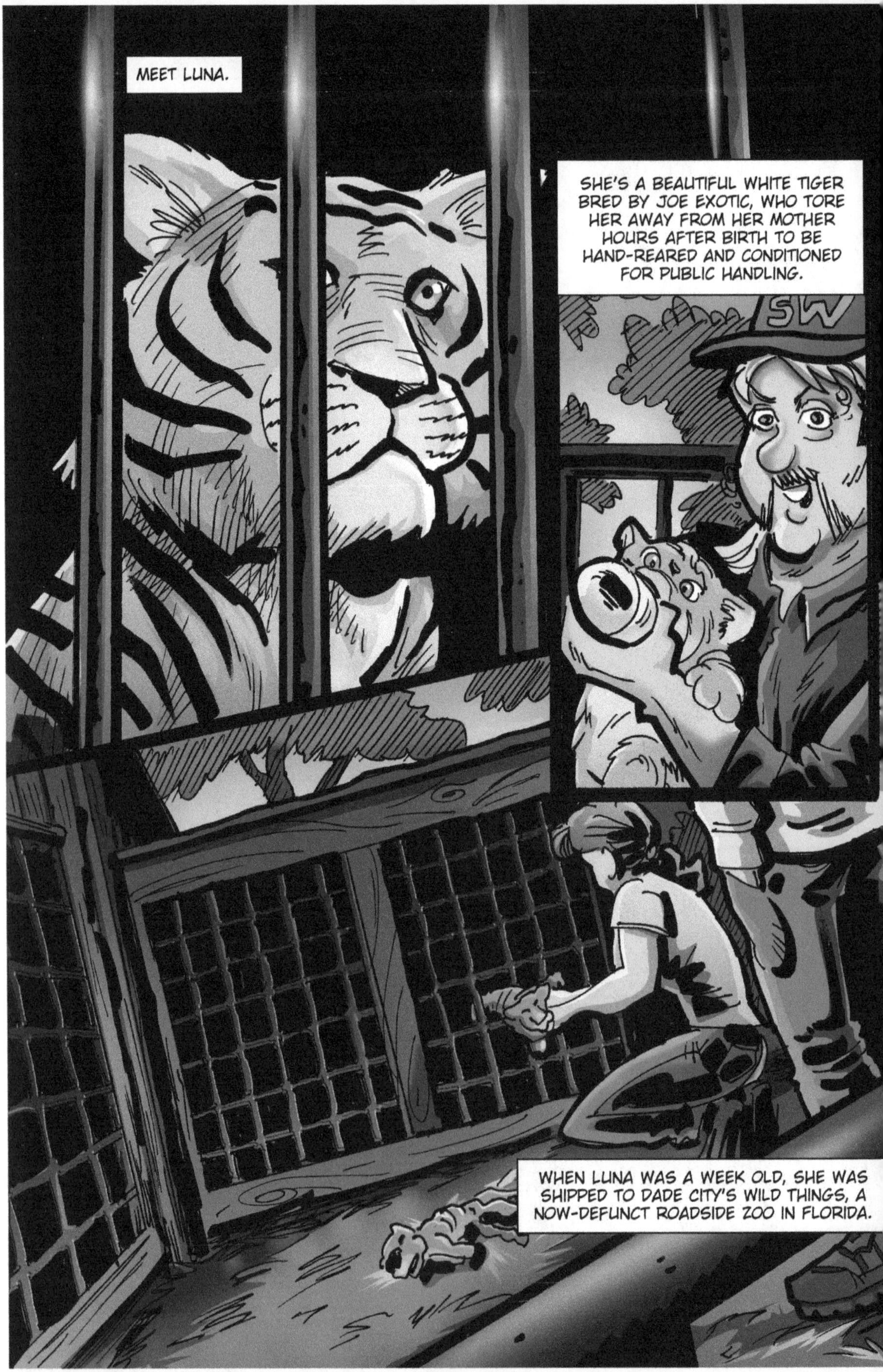
MEET LUNA.
SHE'S A BEAUTIFUL WHITE TIGER BRED BY JOE EXOTIC, WHO TORE HER AWAY FROM HER MOTHER HOURS AFTER BIRTH TO BE HAND-REARED AND CONDITIONED FOR PUBLIC HANDLING.
SW
WHEN LUNA WAS A WEEK OLD, SHE WAS SHIPPED TO DADE CITY'S WILD THINGS, A NOW-DEFUNCT ROADSIDE ZOO IN FLORIDA.

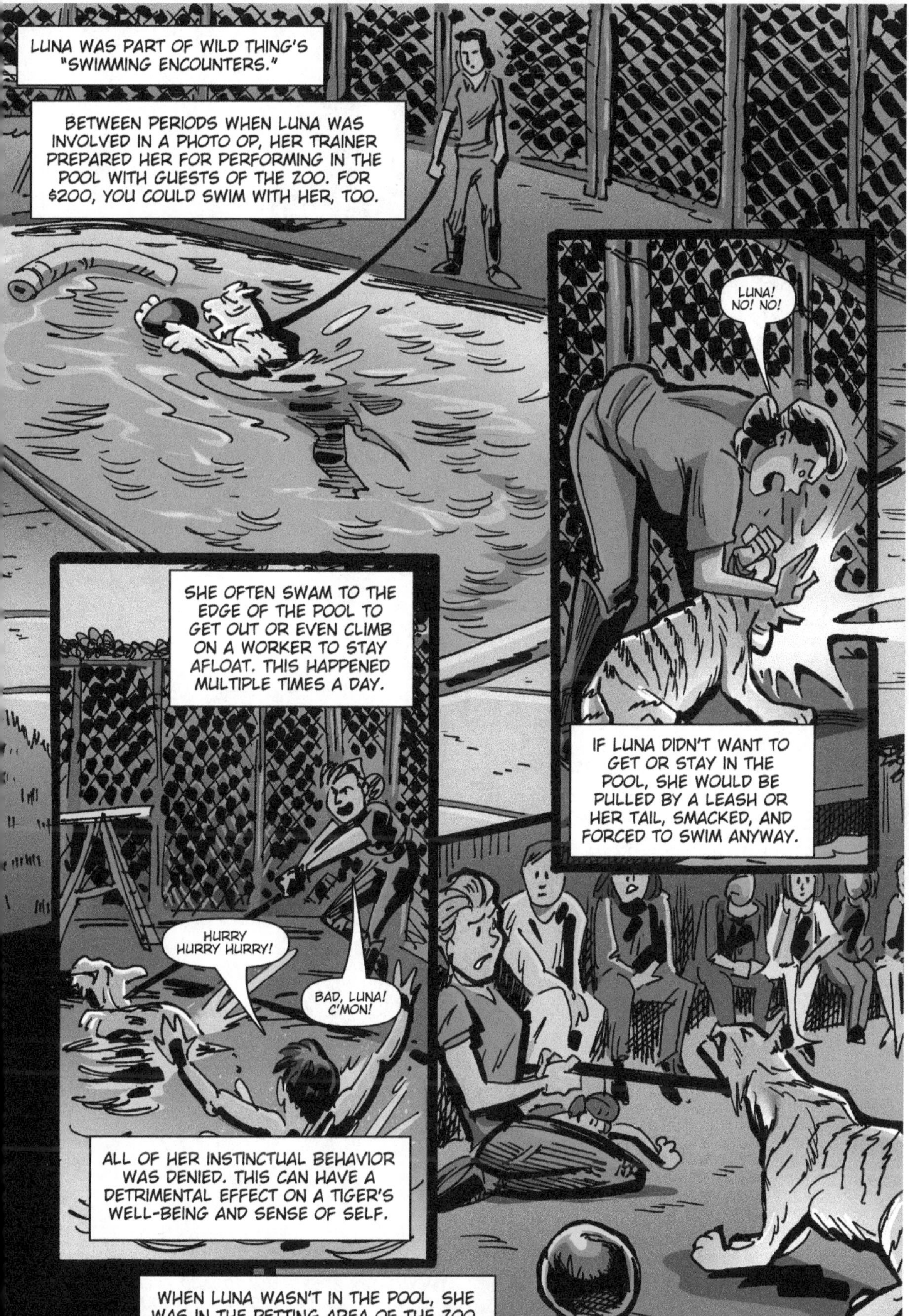
LUNA WAS PART OF WILD THING'S "SWIMMING ENCOUNTERS."
BETWEEN PERIODS WHEN LUNA WAS INVOLVED IN A PHOTO OP, HER TRAINER PREPARED HER FOR PERFORMING IN THE POOL WITH GUESTS OF THE ZOO. FOR $200, YOU COULD SWIM WITH HER, TOO.
LUNA! NO! NO!
IF LUNA DIDN'T WANT TO GET OR STAY IN THE POOL, SHE WOULD BE PULLED BY A LEASH OR HER TAIL, SMACKED, AND FORCED TO SWIM ANYWAY.
SHE OFTEN SWAM TO THE EDGE OF THE POOL TO GET OUT OR EVEN CLIMB ON A WORKER TO STAY AFLOAT. THIS HAPPENED MULTIPLE TIMES A DAY.
HURRY HURRY HURRY!
BAD, LUNA! C'MON!
ALL OF HER INSTINCTUAL BEHAVIOR WAS DENIED. THIS CAN HAVE A DETRIMENTAL EFFECT ON A TIGER'S WELL-BEING AND SENSE OF SELF.
WHEN LUNA WASN'T IN THE POOL, SHE WAS IN THE PETTING AREA OF THE ZOO.
SHE DIDN'T ALWAYS LIKE IT, EITHER.

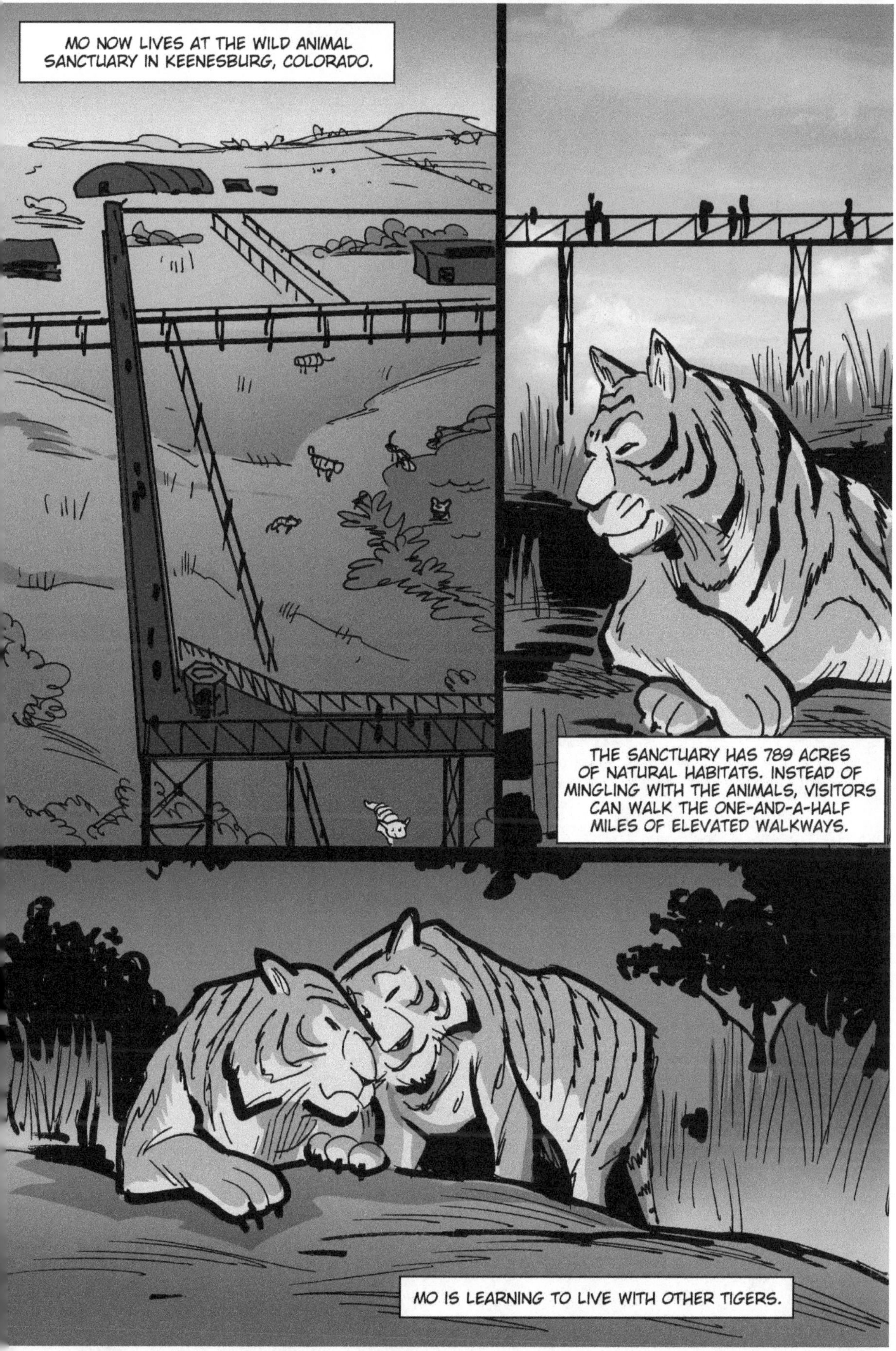
MO NOW LIVES AT THE WILD ANIMAL SANCTUARY IN KEENESBURG, COLORADO.
THE SANCTUARY HAS 789 ACRES OF NATURAL HABITATS. INSTEAD OF MINGLING WITH THE ANIMALS, VISITORS CAN WALK THE ONE-AND-A-HALF MILES OF ELEVATED WALKWAYS.
MO IS LEARNING TO LIVE WITH OTHER TIGERS.

BONUS

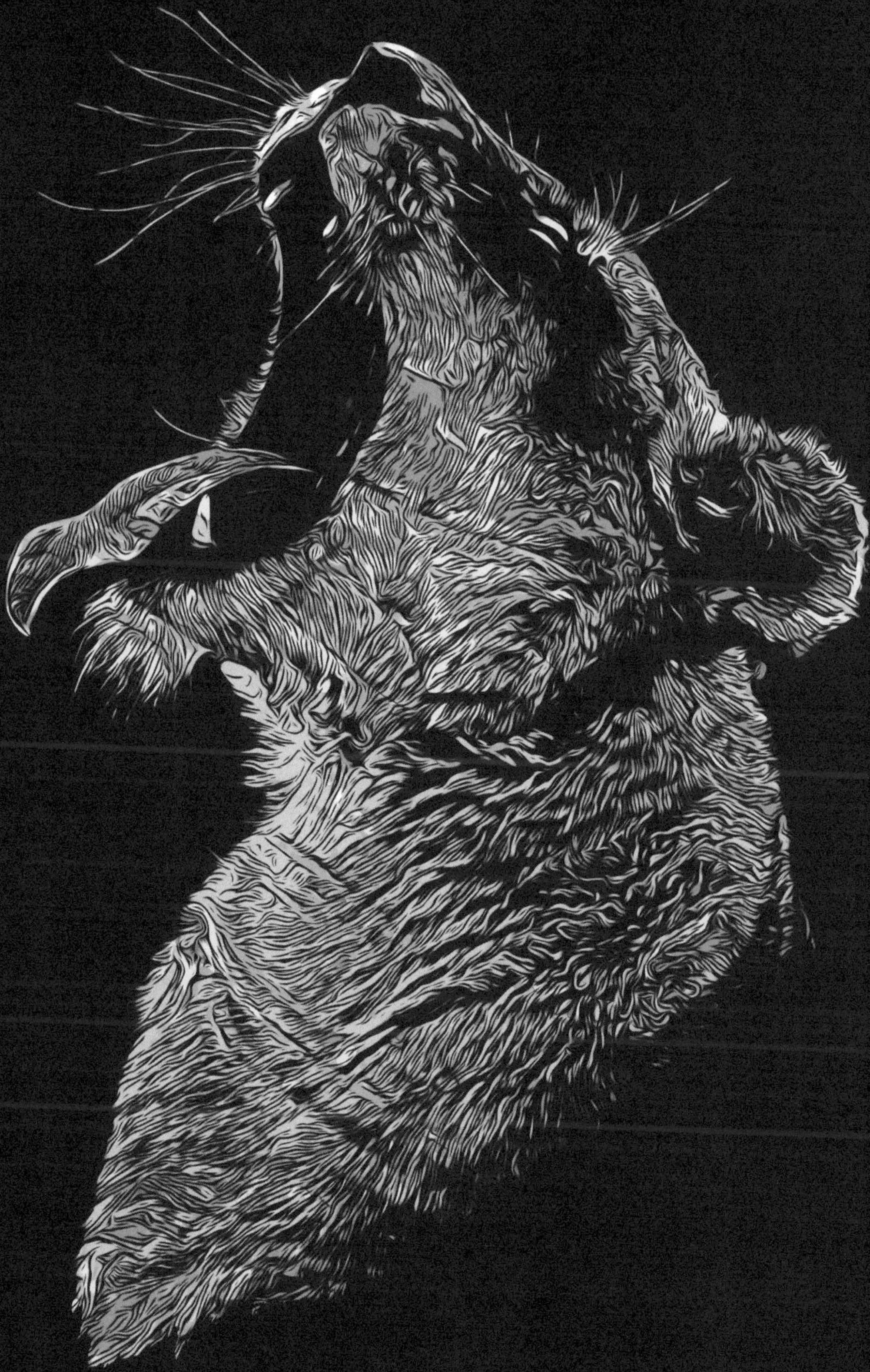

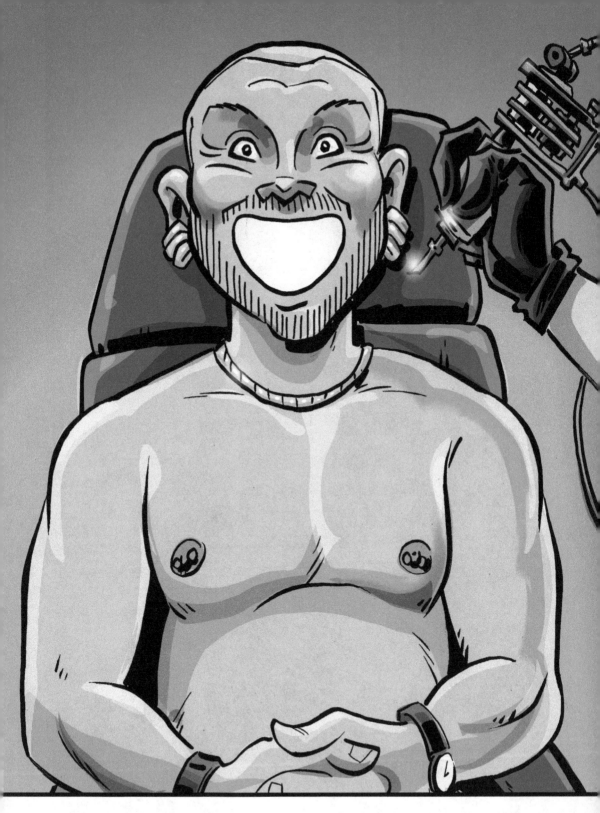

You can draw new teeth & tatts for John Finlay -
Get Creative!

Joe Exotic left you
a **SECRET MESSAGE!**
Can you find it?

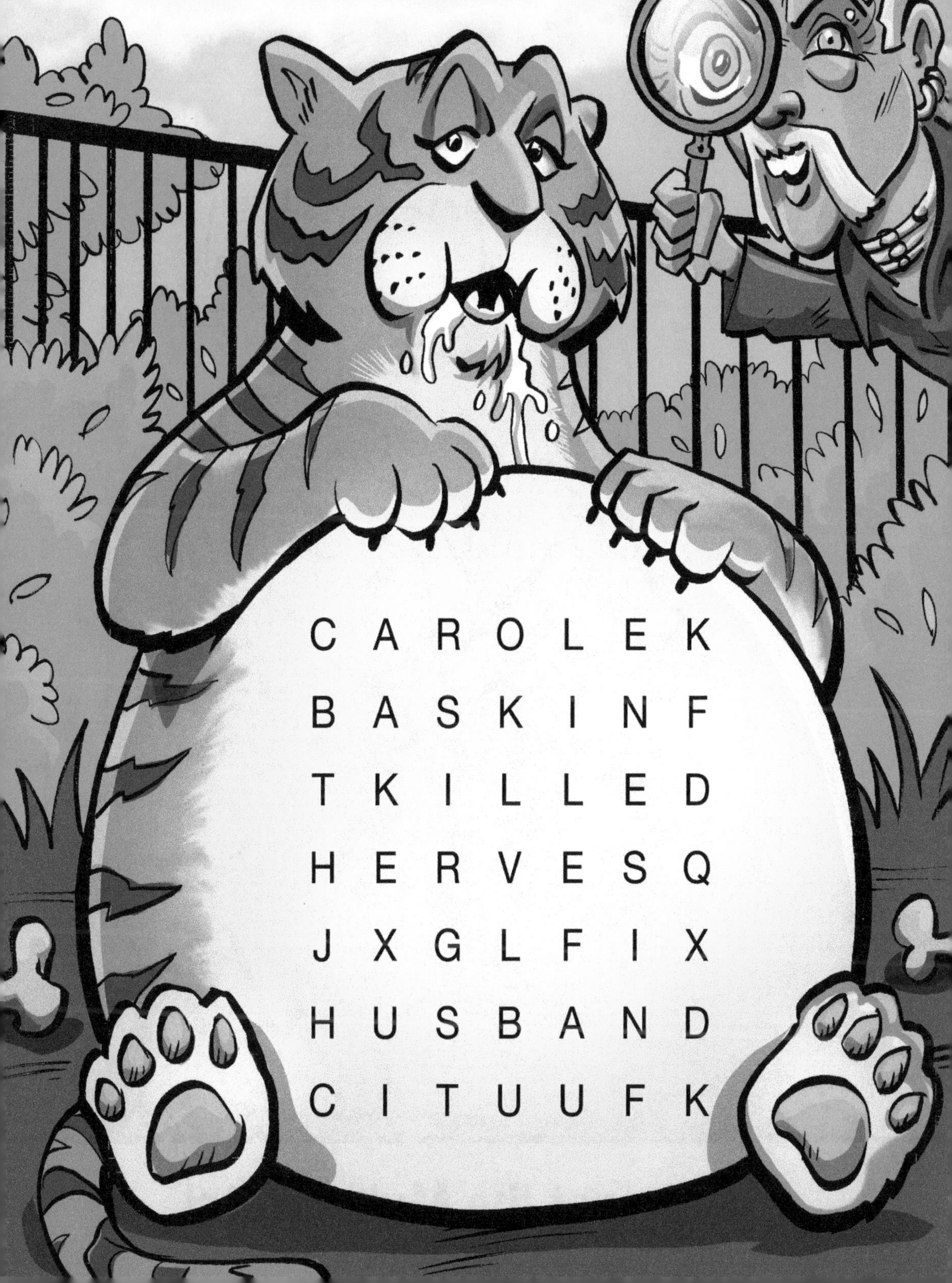
C A R O L E K
B A S K I N F
T K I L L E D
H E R V E S Q
J X G L F I X
H U S B A N D
C I T U U F K

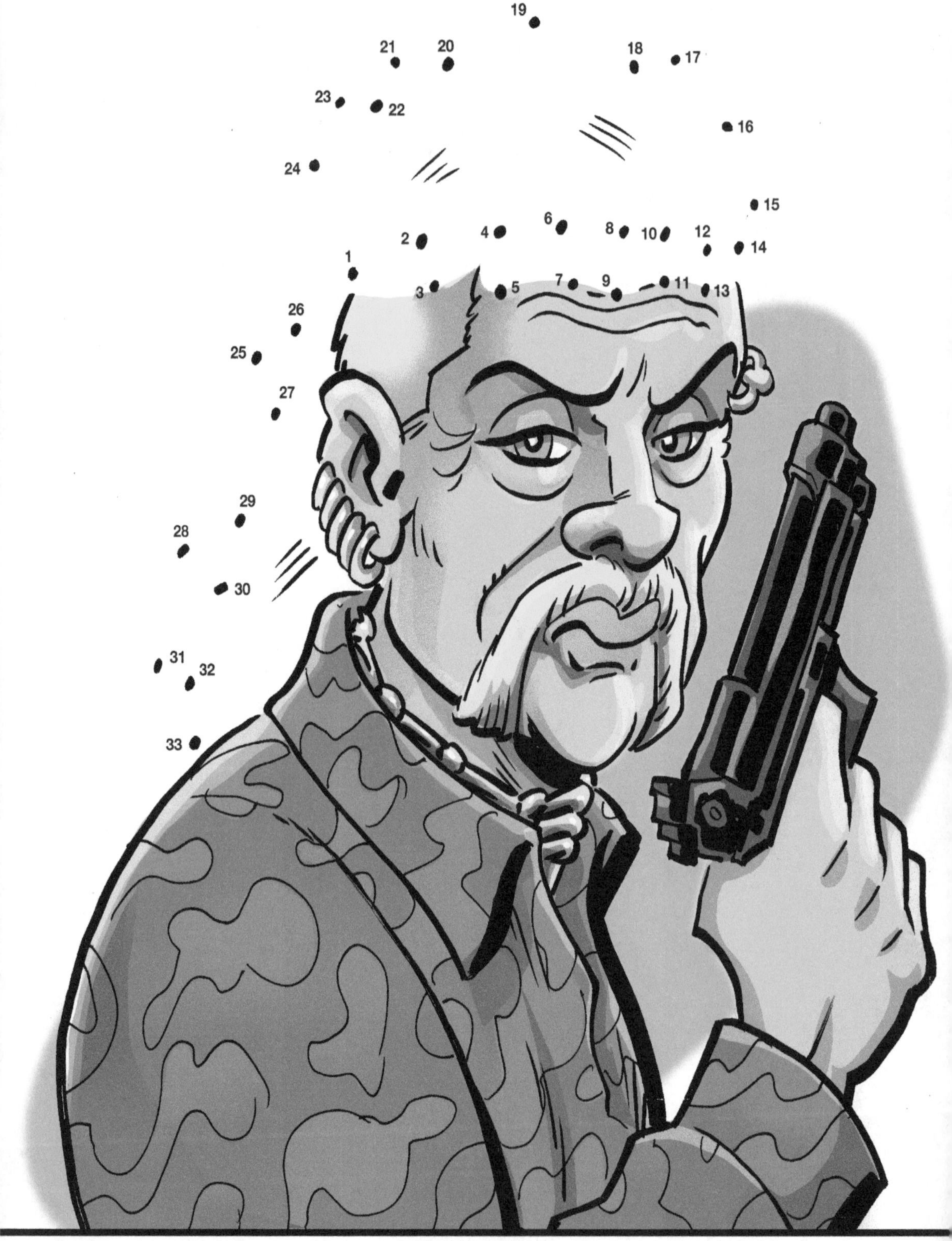

19
21
20
18
17
23
22
16
24
15
6
8
10
12
2
4
14
1
7
9
3
5
11
13
26
25
27
29
28
30
31
32
33

Connect the Mullet dots!

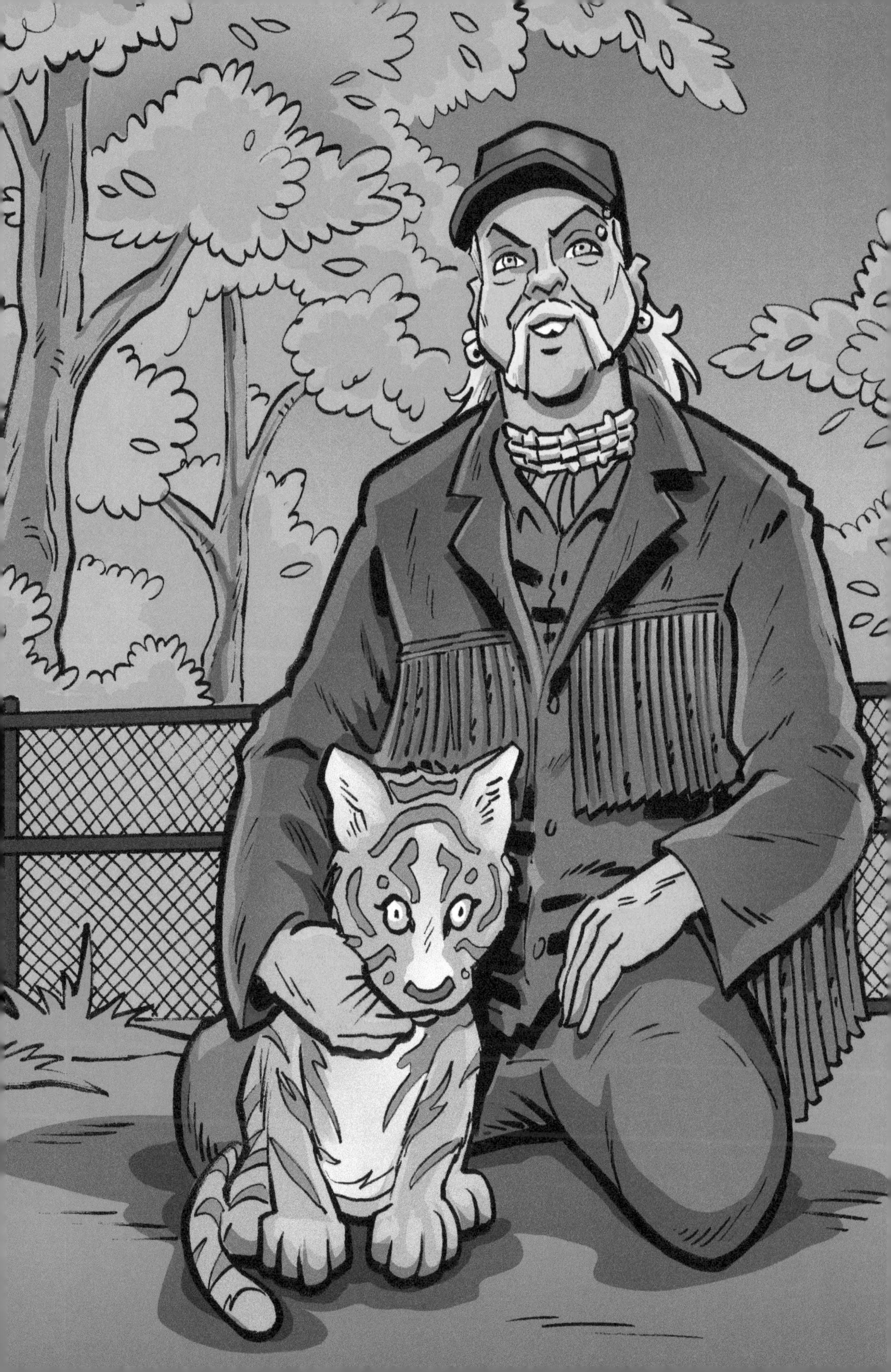

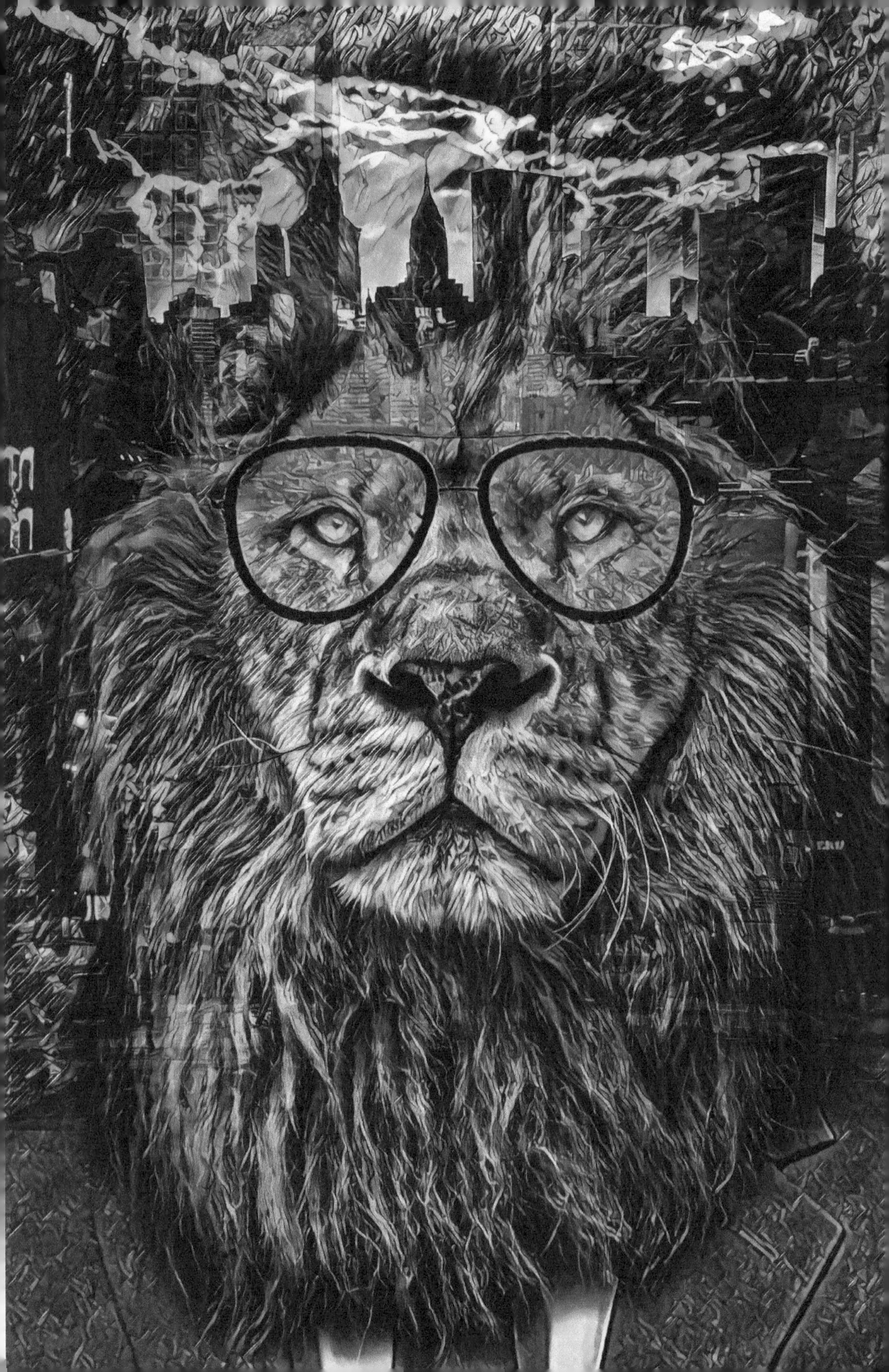

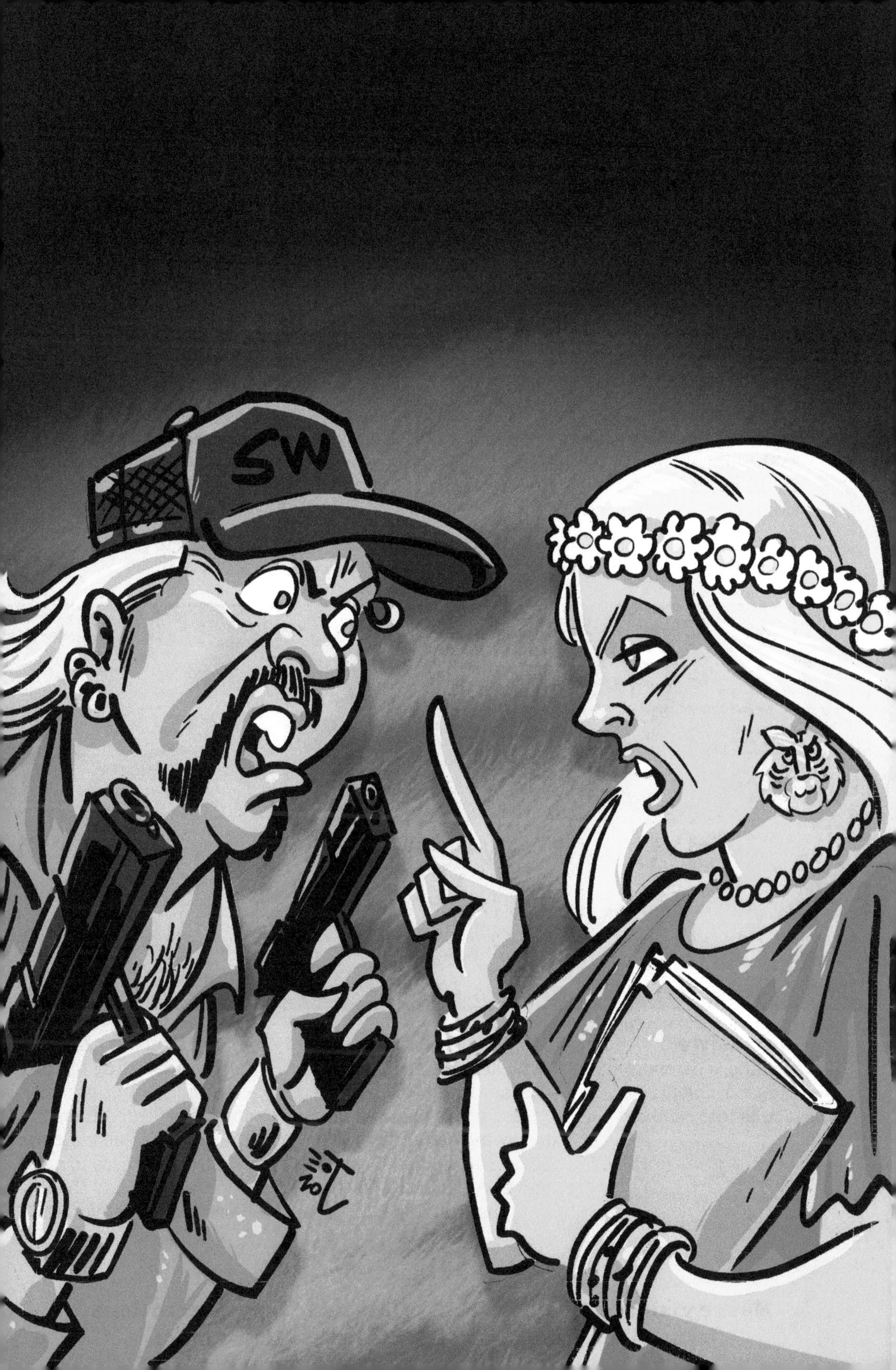
SW

PeTA

Behind the Scenes: PETA's Tiger King Case Files

By Brittany Peet, PETA Foundation Director
of Captive Animal Law Enforcement

By the time I met "Joe Exotic," he'd been on PETA's radar for years. A PETA exposé revealed sick, injured, and dying animals at his facility. Animals were kicked, deprived of food, blasted with pressurized hoses and fire extinguishers, and beaten with the blunt end of a gun. We documented that operations like Joe's tear infant tiger cubs away from their mothers and then relegate them to cramped cages after they're too old to use as photo props. In response to our long-running campaign, Joe shot and hanged "PETA" in effigy and even threatened me by name on his show.

PETA eventually rescued almost 50 animals from his facility and got them placed in reputable sanctuaries—two of them were the chimpanzees featured at the end of Tiger King. They had lived in separate cages at Joe's roadside zoo for 10 years. When they were introduced during their first week at the sanctuary, they hugged for hours.

When I met Joe in 2017, he was falling out with Jeff Lowe and eager to give me the dirt on every tiger terrorizer he knew:

Jeff Lowe	**Tim Stark**	**"Doc" Antle**
Joe's business partner, got caught smuggling big-cat cubs into casinos.	who acquired cubs from Joe, admitted to beating a leopard to death and declawing baby tigers. The USDA revoked his license, and in April 2020, he lost his first appeal.	who according to Joe also acquired tiger cubs from him, sometimes kills the cubs who've outgrown their usefulness in a gas chamber and then cremates them on site.

How You Can Help:

Never visit any business that offers hands-on interactions with wild animals. Visit PETA.org to learn more.

Joe "Exotic" is behind bars—but other animal exploiters are still in business:

At Waccatee Zoo in South Carolina, a tiger named Lila has lost most
of her fur and spends her days in a cramped, barren cell.
Behind bars in roadside zoos across the country, animals like her—including
big cats, bears, and baboons—have nothing to do all day but pace
endlessly, rock back and forth, and even engage in self-mutilation.
PETA has rescued 75 big cats, 73 bears, and 15 primates,
who now live in true sanctuaries.
To learn more and to support PETA's work
to help these animals, visit **PETA.org**.

DON'T Stop at Roadside Zoos!

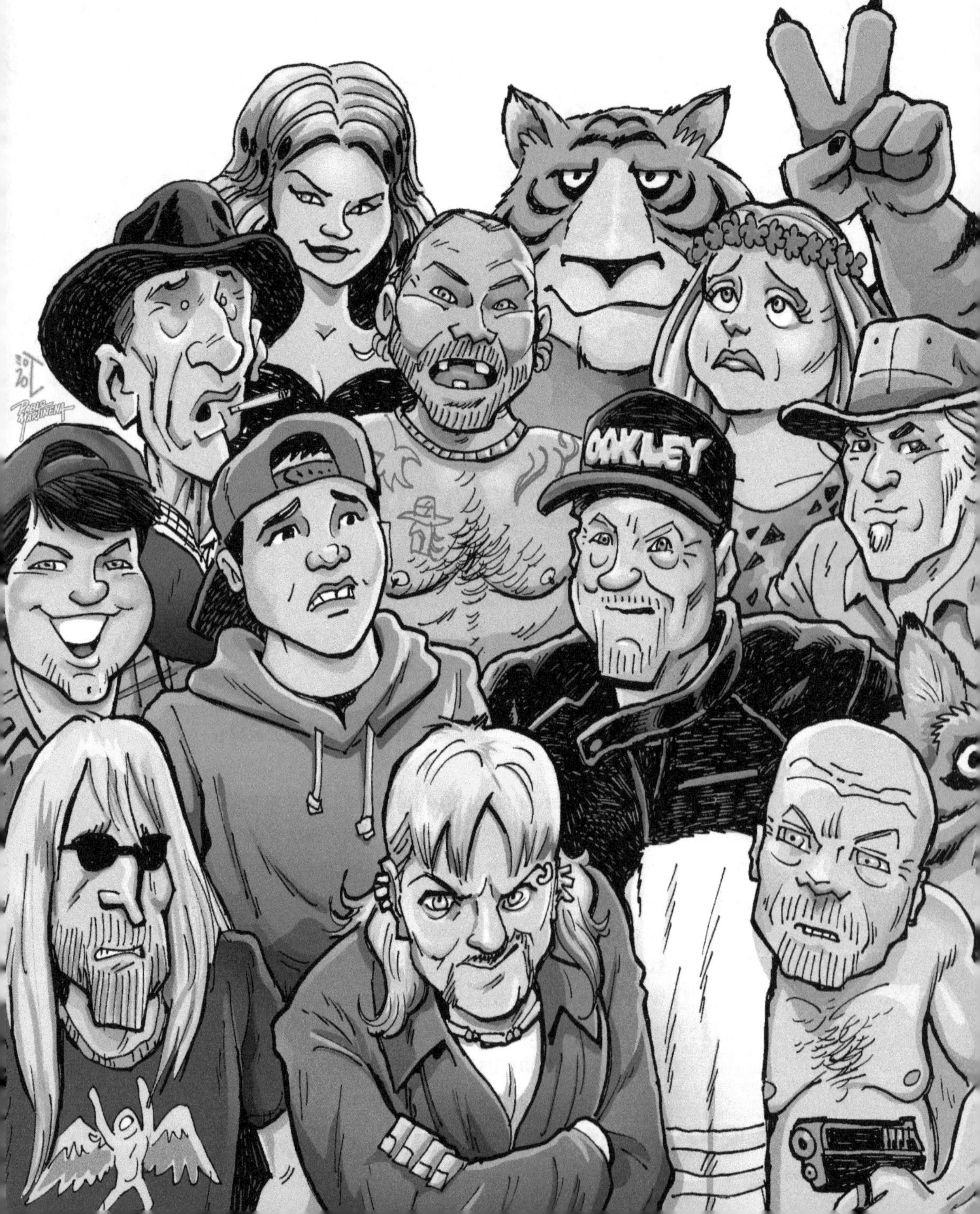
OAKLEY

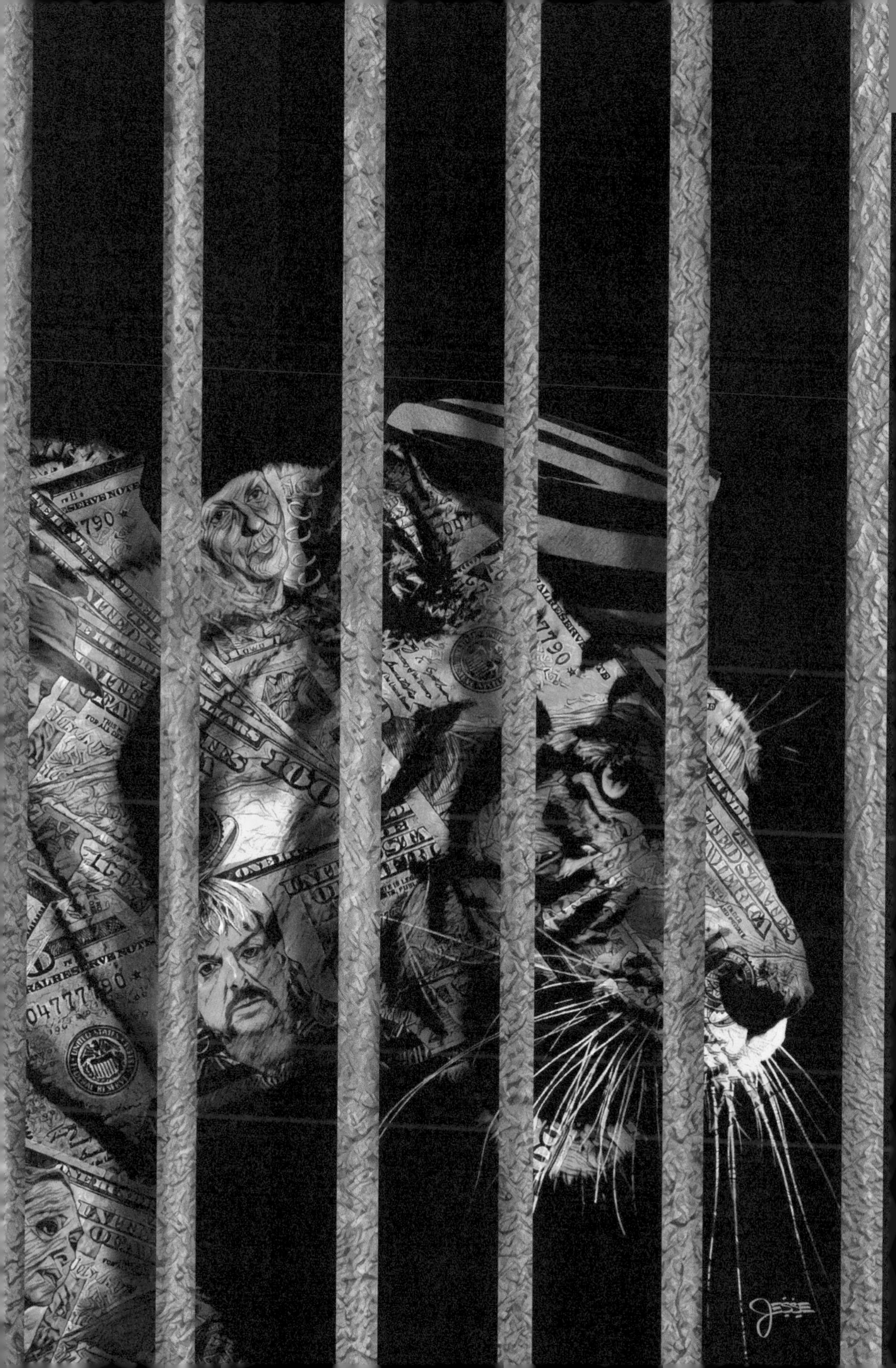

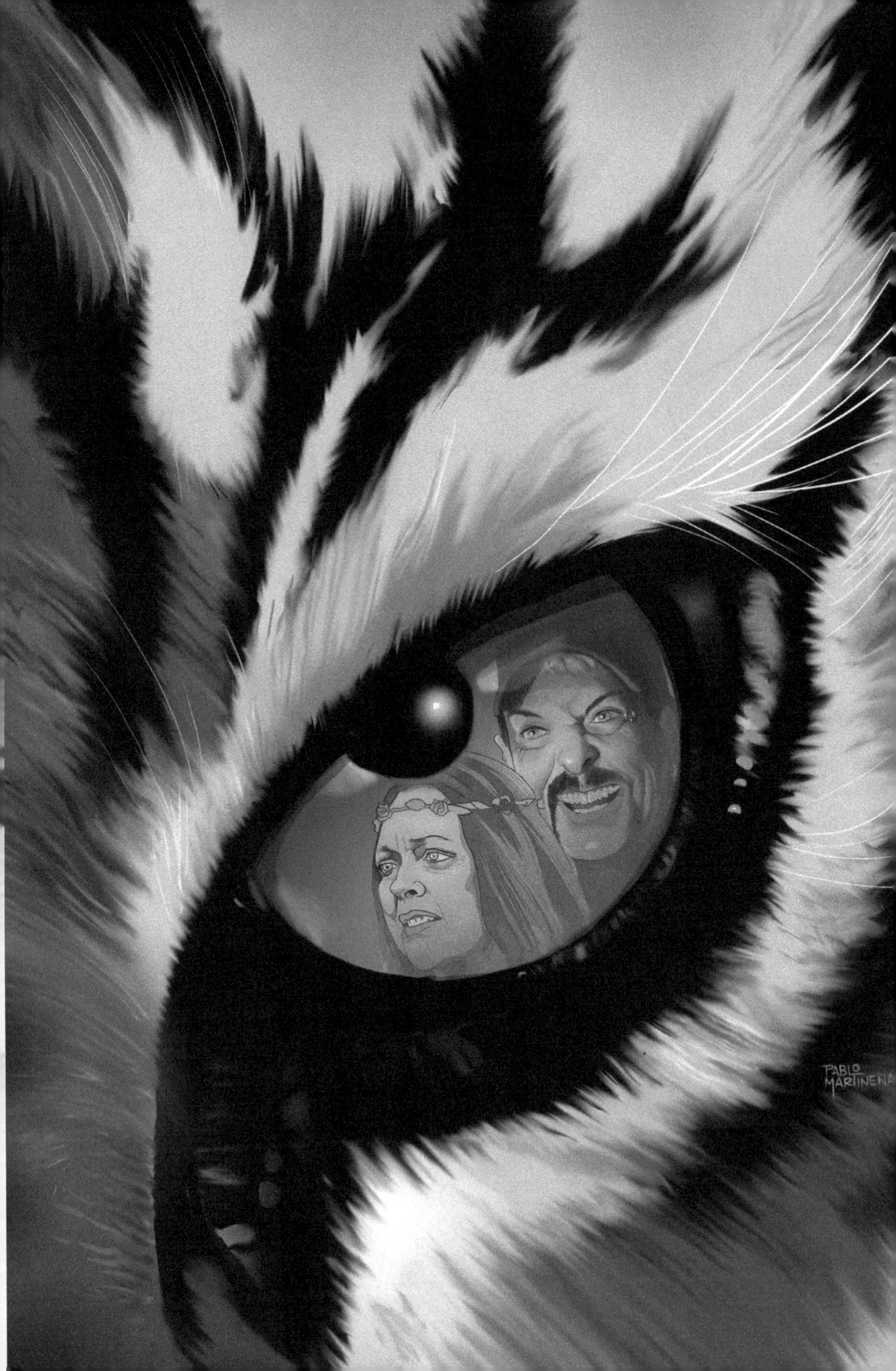
PABLO MARTINENA

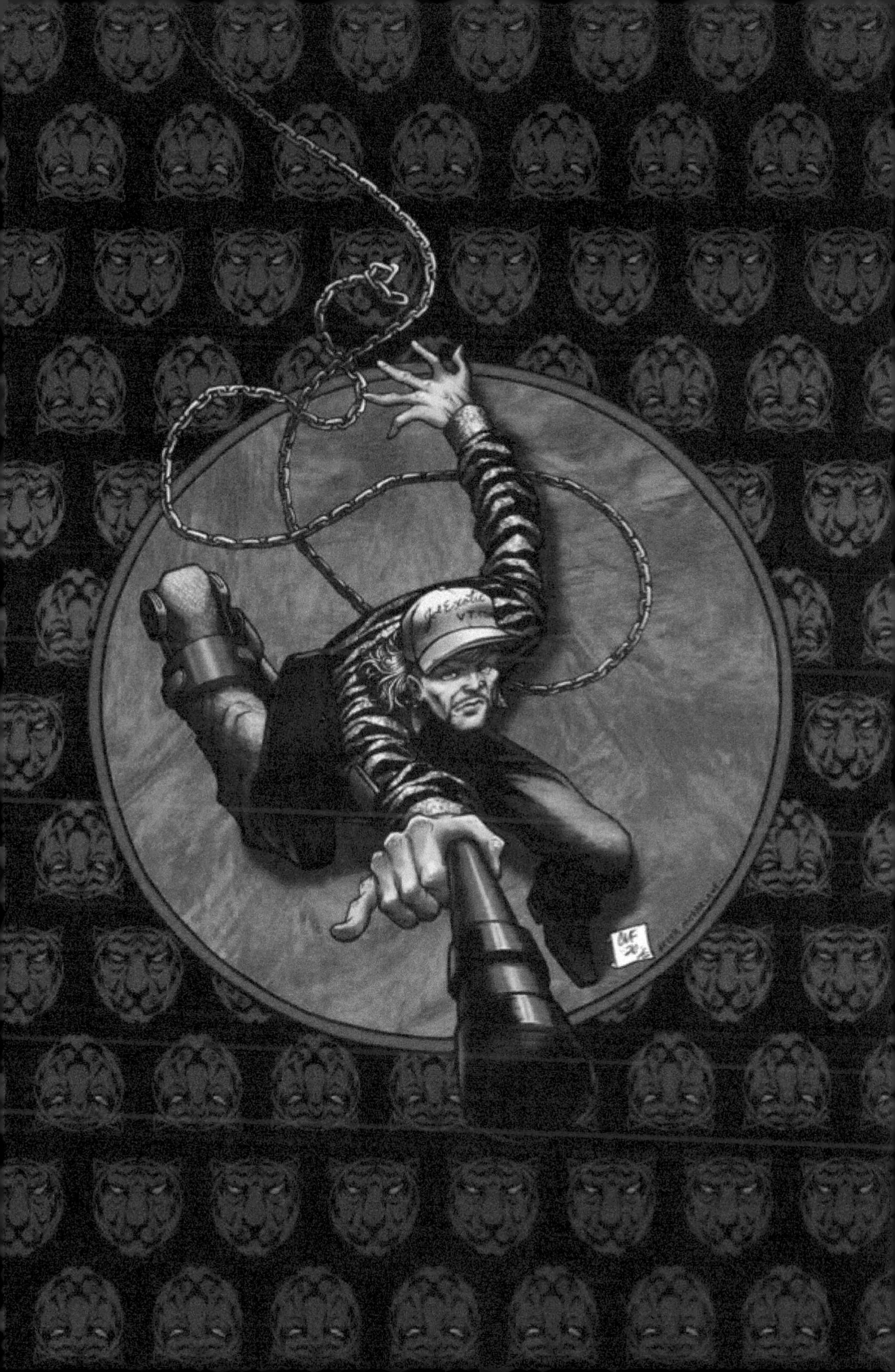

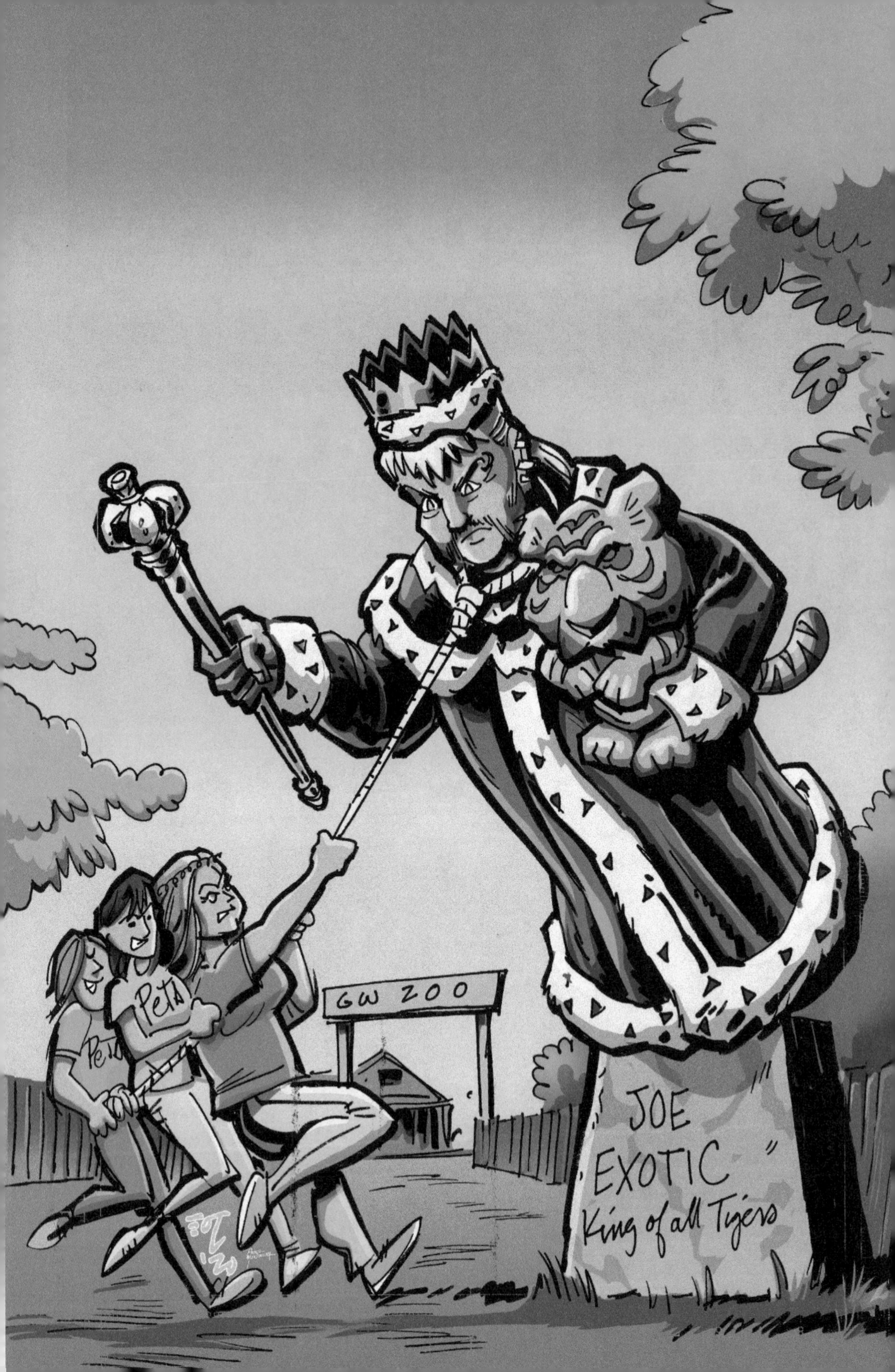
GW ZOO
JOE EXOTIC
King of all Tygers
PETA
PETA

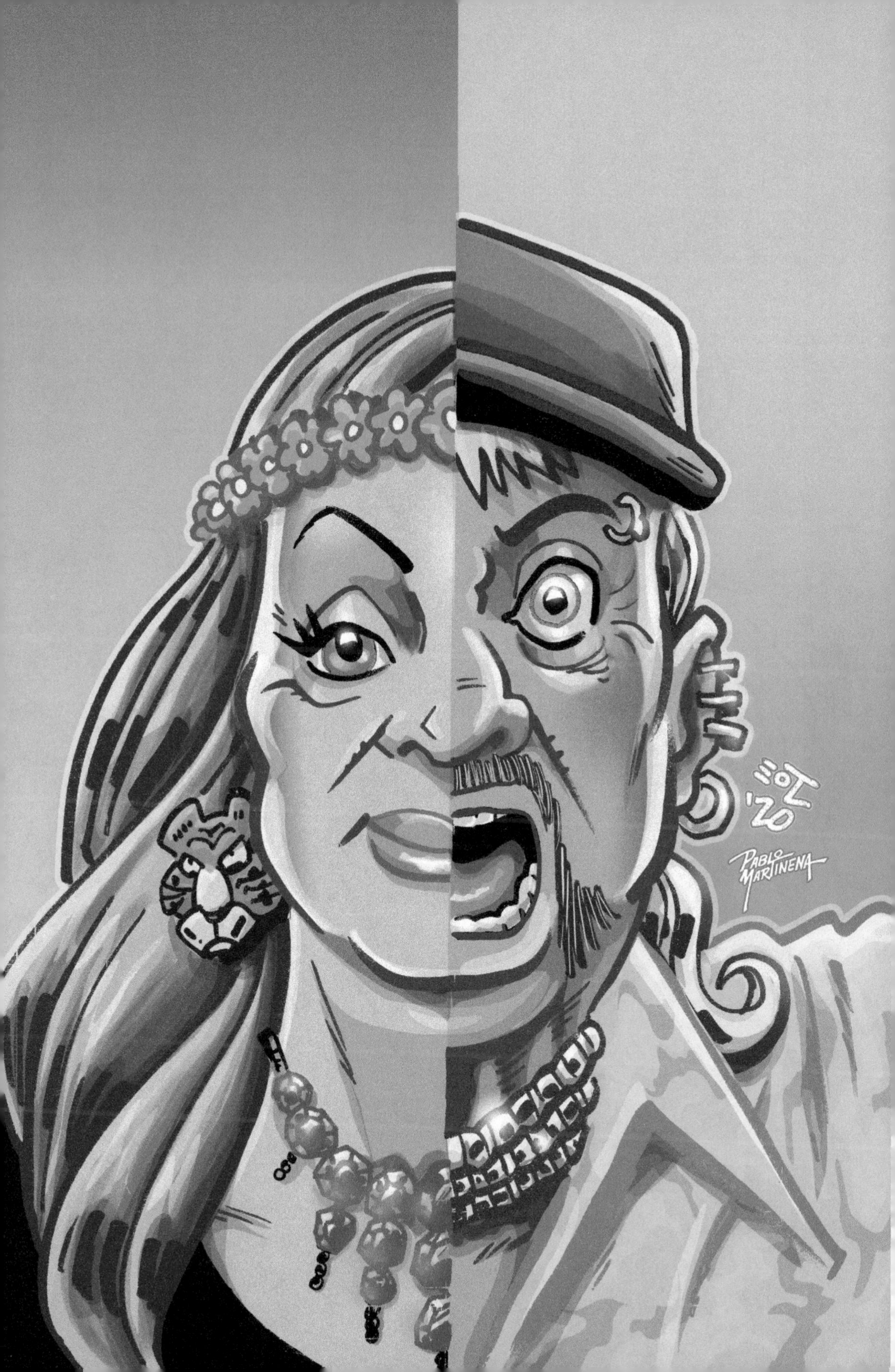
'20
PABLO MARTINENA

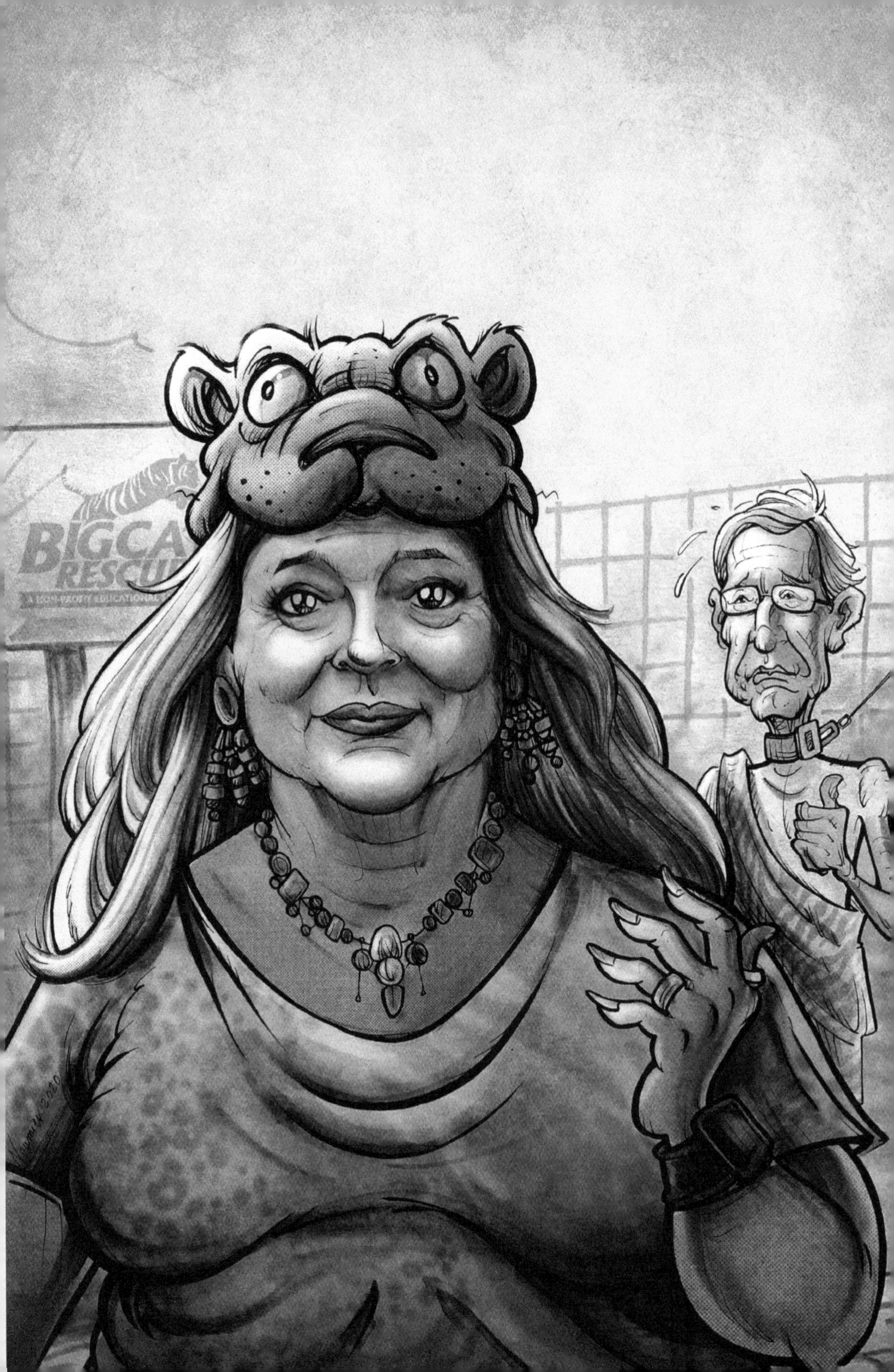
BIGCA
RESCU

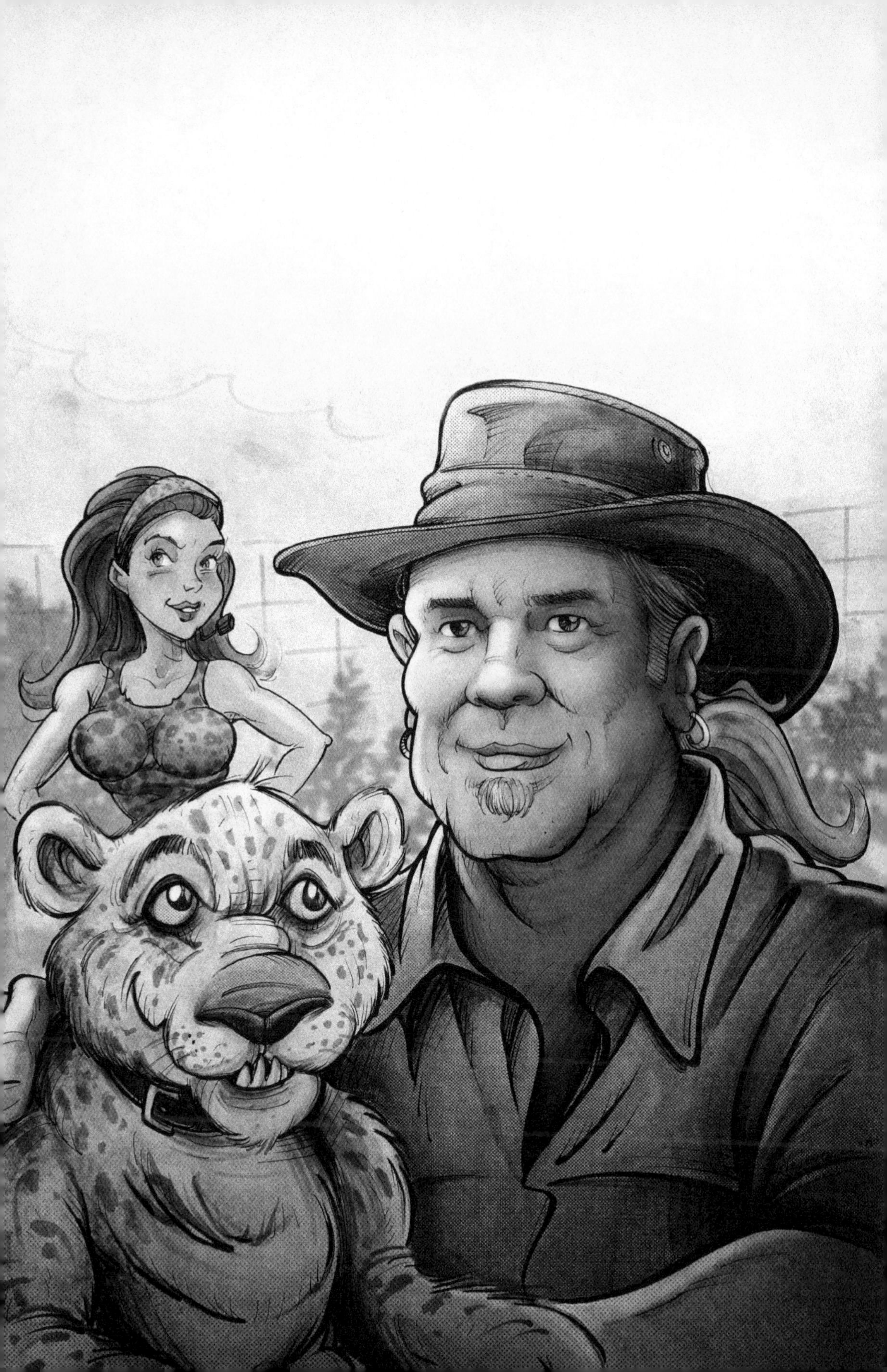

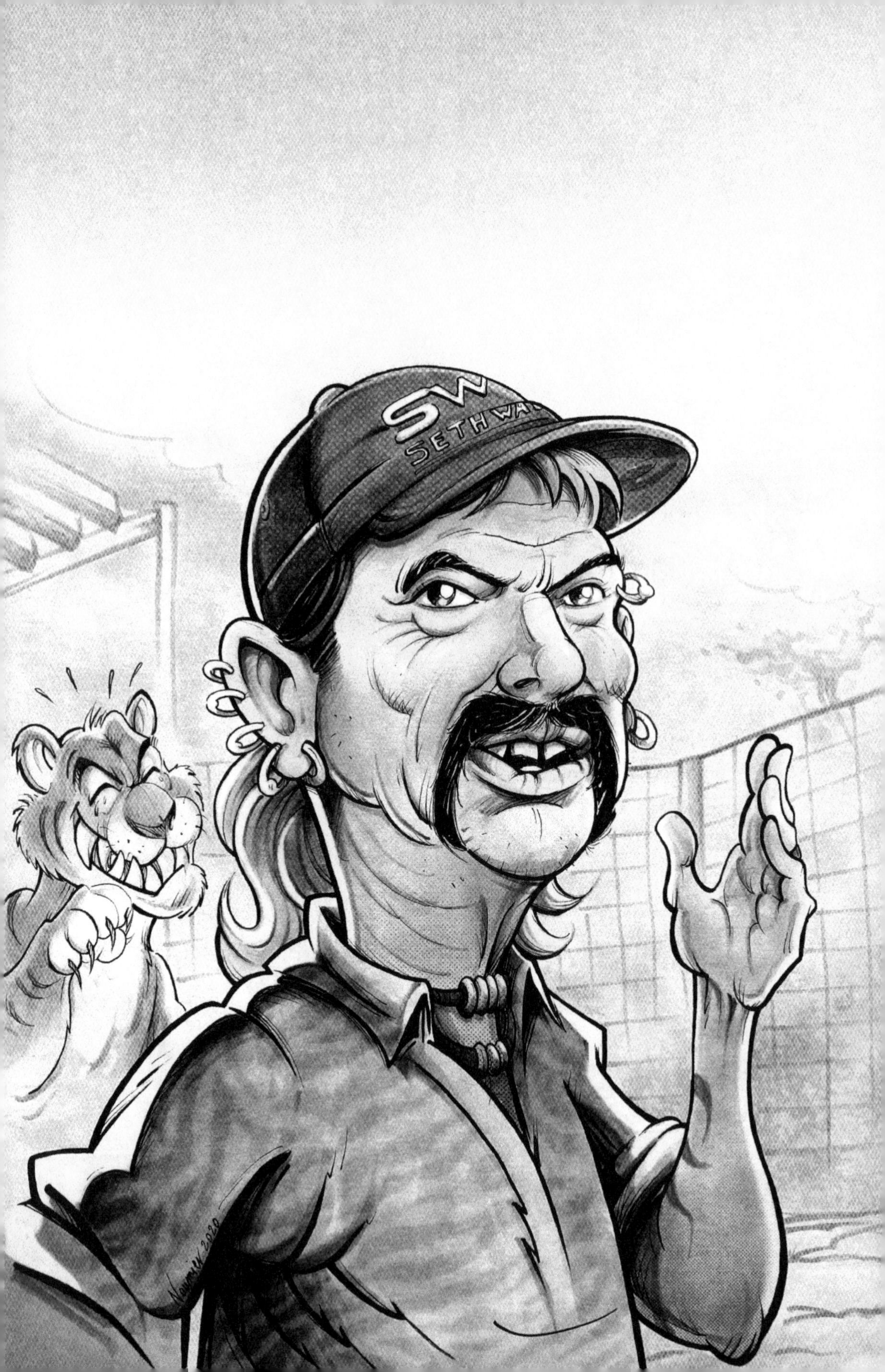
SW
SETH WA

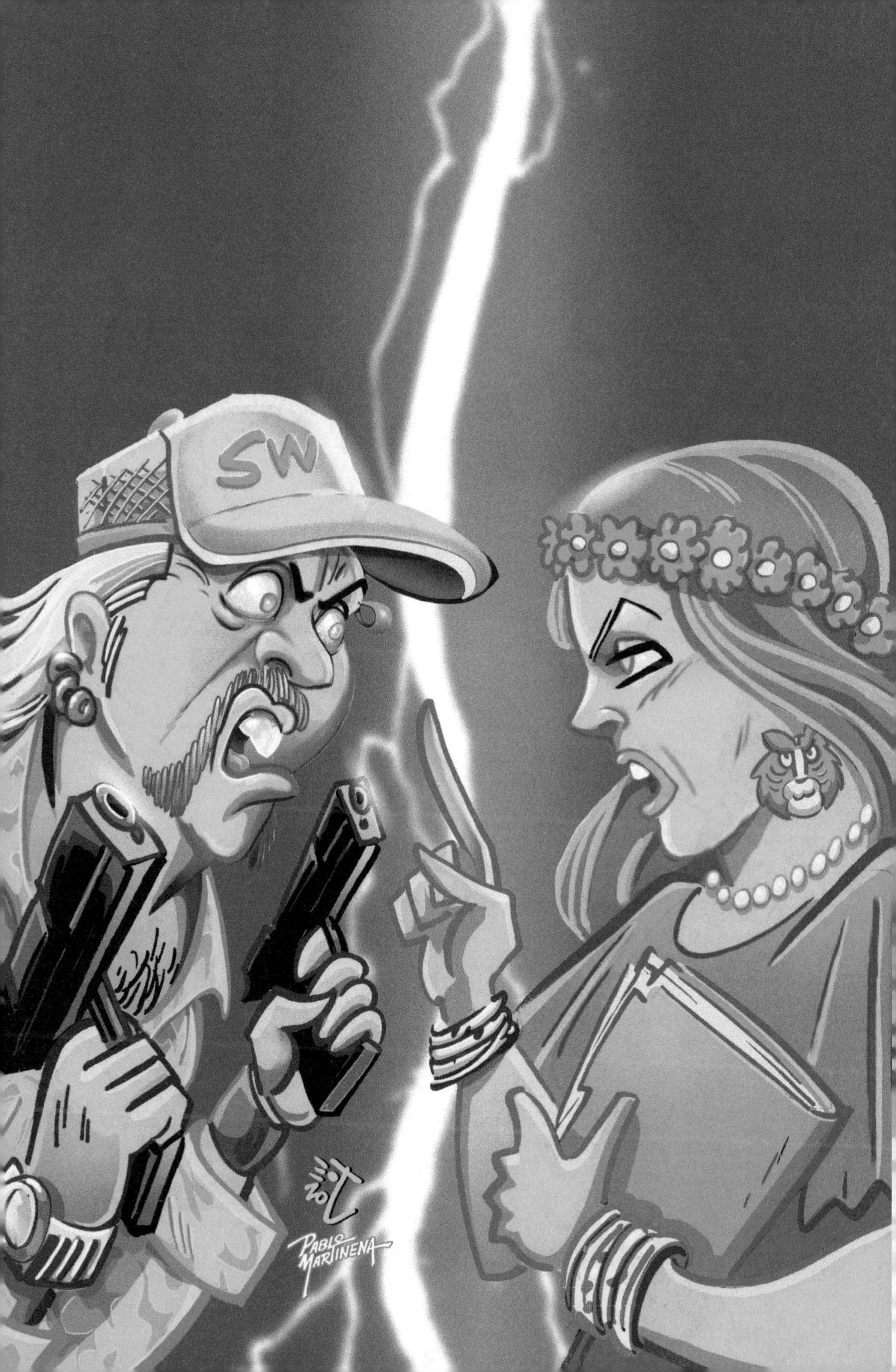
SW
PABLO MARTINENA

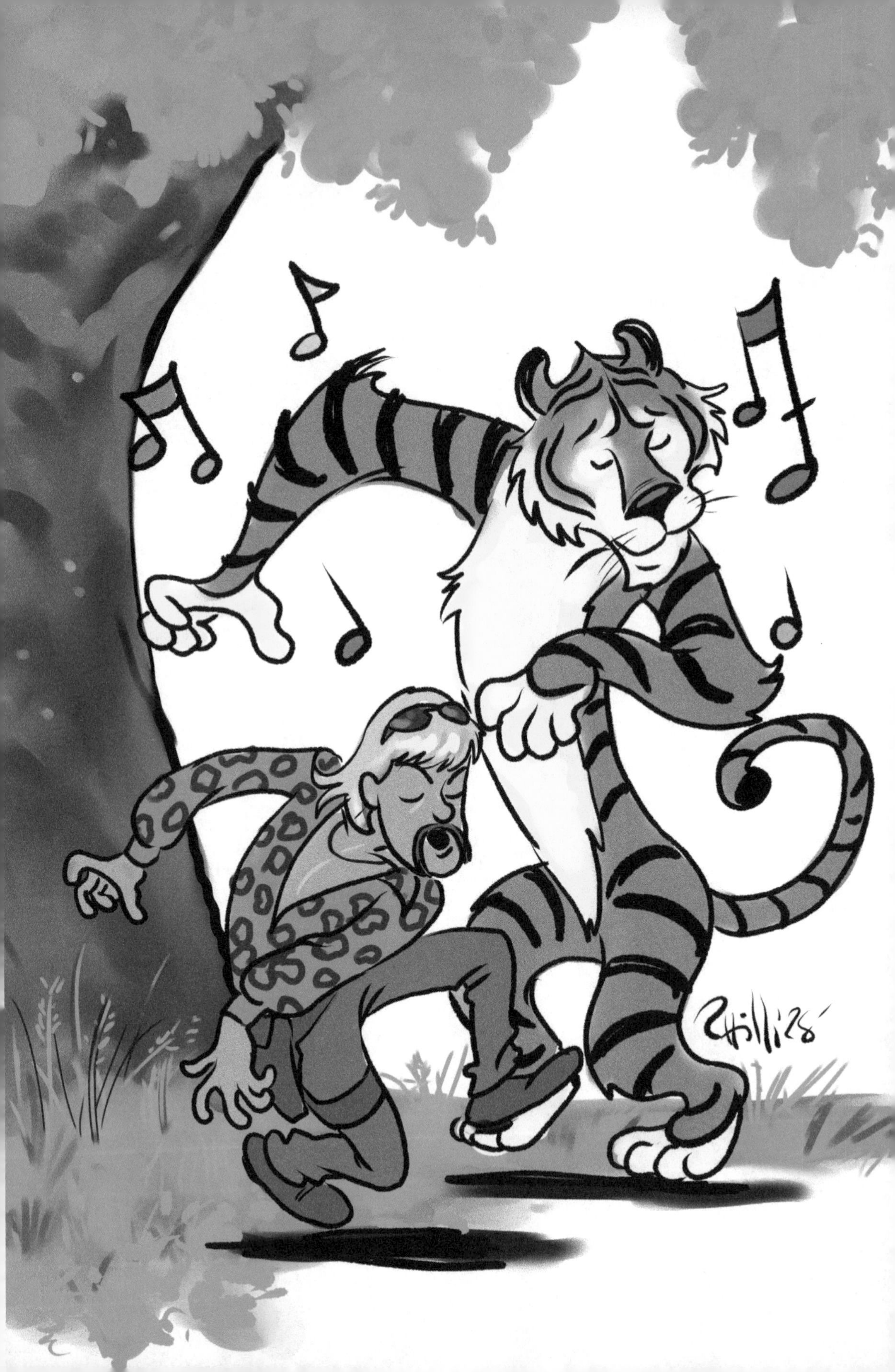

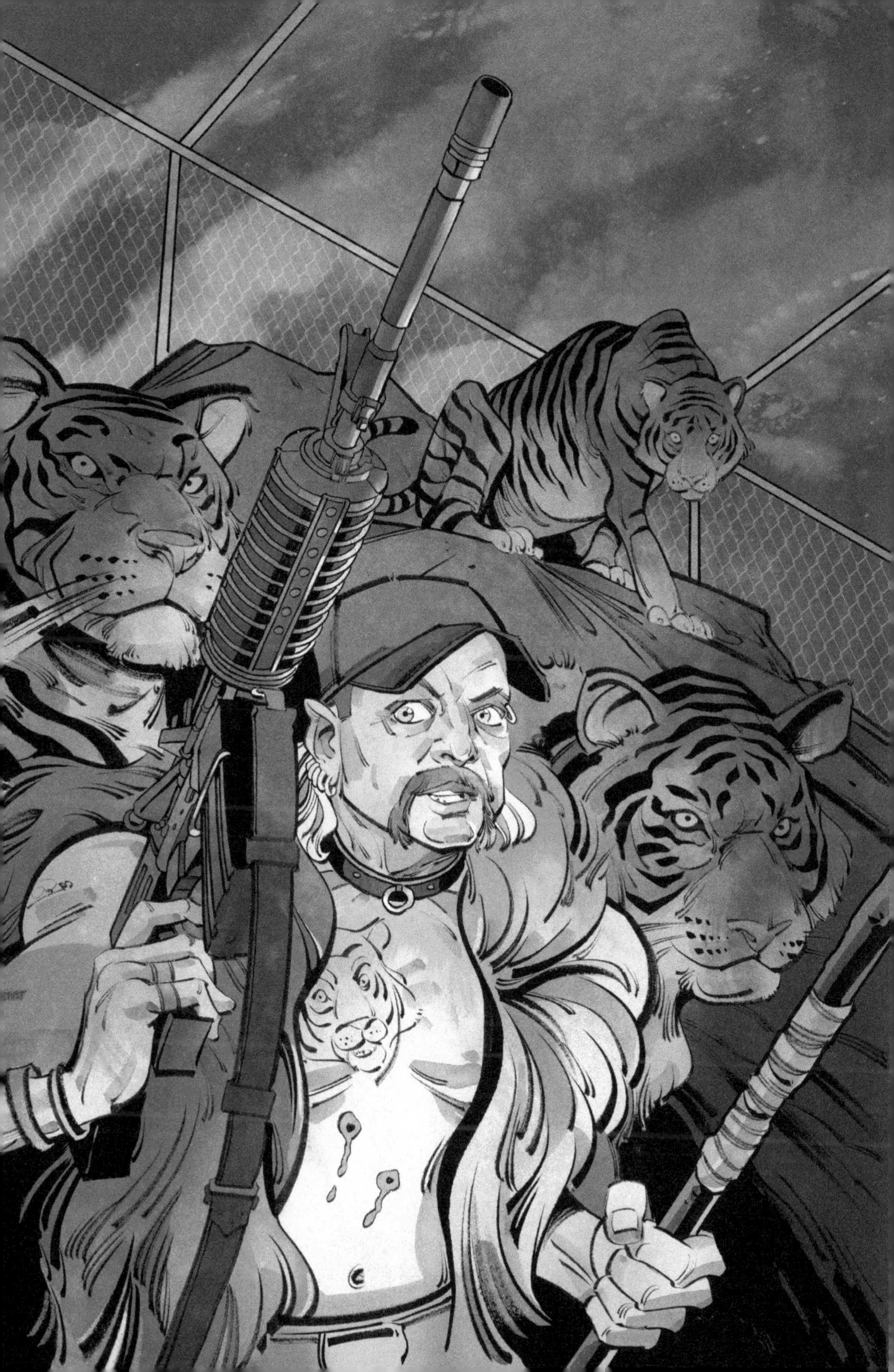

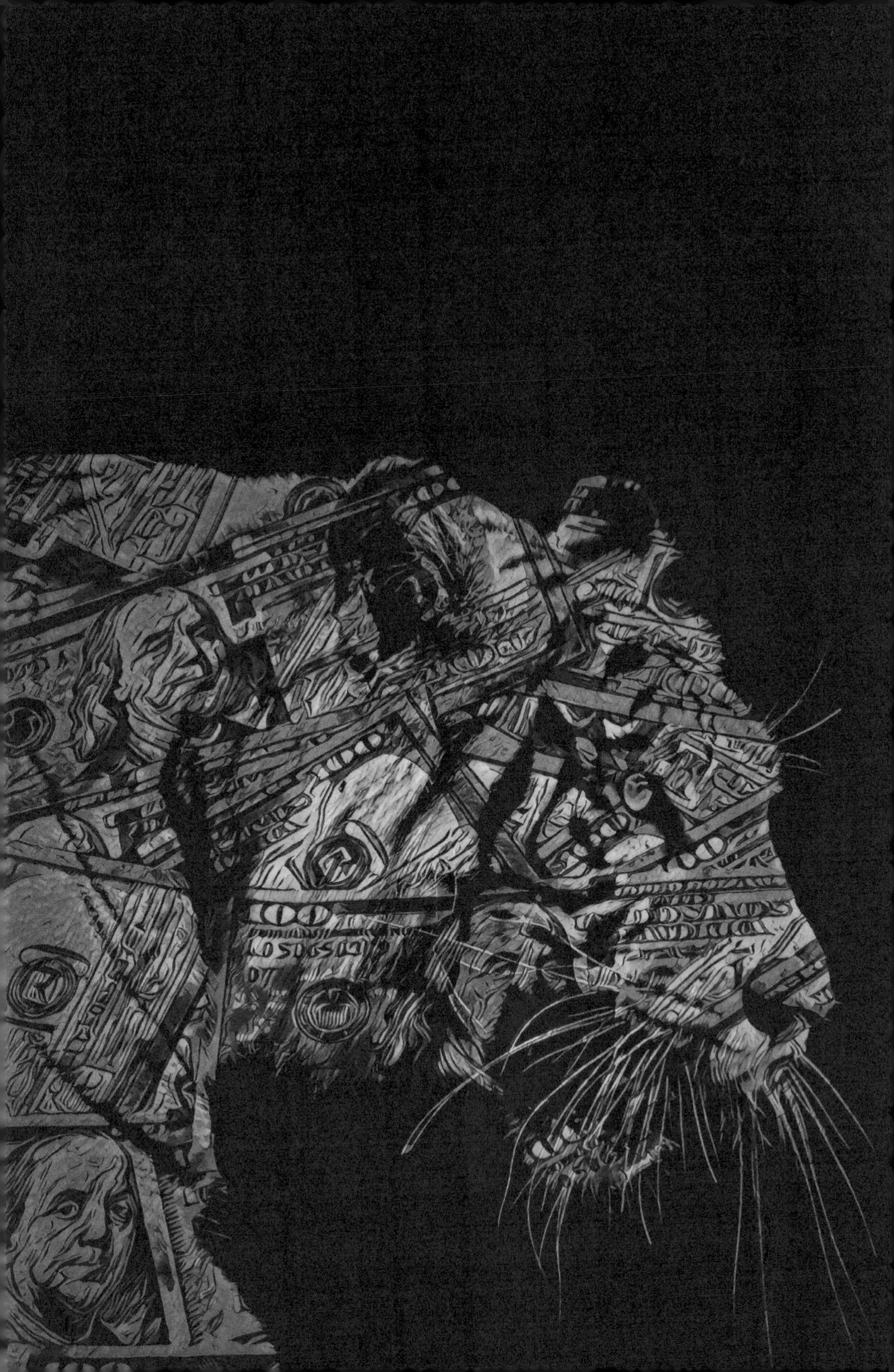

Special thanks to: PeTA & Jesse Johnson

INFAMOUS
TIGER KING

Michael Frizell	Writer
Joe Paradise	Art
Pablo Martinena	Colors
Ben Glibert	Letters
Joe Paradise	Cover

Pin-Ups: Joe Phillips, Noumier Tawilah, Jesse Johnson, Joe Paradise & Kagan McLoud

Darren G. Davis — Editor

Darren G. Davis
Publisher

Maggie Jessup
Publicity

Susan Ferris
Entertainment Manager